ABOUT THE AUTHOR

Heidi Tucker won the 2017 Illumination Award for her first inspirational book *Finding Hope in the Journey*. Her passion for writing and speaking about light and hope has inspired thousands. Heidi is known as a gifted storyteller who motivates us to rise up and find power within. Her messages help us recognize truth and make a difference.

When Heidi isn't writing her next book or speaking at a conference, you'll find her spending time outdoors with her husband, four grown children and eight grandchildren. She loves sunflowers, hiking and ice cream … not necessarily in that order.

Find out more about Heidi at ThePickledSunflower.com

Also by Heidi Tucker

2017 Illumination Award
Finding Hope in the Journey

There is hope – glimpses of hope that are unique and divinely meant just for you. We must watch and listen and tune all senses. It is positioning your heart, mind and soul to recognize messages of hope from God.

Available at:

ThePickledSunflower.com
Deseret Book
Amazon.com

ISBN 978-0-996-61461-0

Published by The Pickled Sunflower 2017

Cover Photography by Austin Tucker Media

Cover Design by Dylan Tucker

First Printing

SERVIE'S SONG

Heidi Tucker

DEDICATION:

Servie
For your beautiful heart,
your living example of faith,
your inspirational story,
and your courage in asking me to write it.

My readers
For those who contacted me
after my first book and simply said –
please keep writing.

Their story, yours, mine –
it's what we all carry with us
on this trip we take,
and we owe it to each other
to respect our stories
and learn from them.

William Carlos Williams

TABLE OF CONTENTS

Preface 1

Introduction 5

Chapter One – Shattered Dreams 9

Chapter Two – Divine Nature 19

Chapter Three – Live Your Truth 33

Chapter Four – A Broken Heart 47

Chapter Five – Adjust Your Sails 69

Chapter Six – A Song of Service 87

Chapter Seven – Then Sings My Soul 107

Chapter Eight – One Song 127

Chapter Nine – A Song of Hope 155

Chapter Ten – Your Song 165

"How did you find this story?"

A common question asked of me. The short answer – I didn't find this story. It found me.

I first met Servie at church. I didn't know her well, but I knew she was from Zimbabwe and had recently been attending. I welcomed Servie with a smile and a friendly greeting on Sundays and hoped she felt loved and accepted in our congregation. We didn't really know each other beyond that.

One Sunday Servie found me at church and said she had something she needed to ask me. She asked if I would come to her home the following Tuesday morning. I trusted my gut which told me that I needed to pay this woman a visit.

Two days later, I entered the neighborhood where Servie was living. My schedule was overbooked with travel and speaking engagements from the release of my first book "Finding Hope in the Journey," and I felt rushed and anxious about getting everything done. I grumbled as I considered that I didn't have time for this. When I pulled onto Servie's street, I recognized my heart was not in the right place and so pulled the car over and said a quick prayer. There were words asking for a better attitude and a sincere desire to help Servie with whatever she felt was important enough to ask me in person.

Servie welcomed me with her famous big smile and warm hug. We took a seat at the table in the living room. I noticed her scriptures were open. We talked about the weather and anything else you do to break the ice. Finally, I spoke up.

"Servie, what can I do to help you?" I said.

"I don't even know how to ask you," she replied. Her eyes glistened with emotion.

"Servie you can ask me anything – anything," I pleaded.

I wondered if there was trouble. Wondered if she needed some service from church members. I really didn't know, but felt a strong desire to serve this kind woman.

She began to tell me that much had happened in her life. Much sorrow. Terrible heartache. But that she had once again found joy in learning about the gospel. And she knew *for sure* that God answers prayers. She said that she had very strong feelings from God that she needed to tell her story, but she was uneducated and unable to write.

I listened intently – still not sure where this was going. My heart began to pound.

"I have prayed and prayed to God asking how I am to do this," Servie said quietly. "When I saw you at church last month, you were reading a Christmas story to the ladies. I saw a light on your face. It was God answering my prayers. He was telling me I needed to ask you to help me write my story. Will you help me?"

I was stunned. Tears filled my eyes. I felt a powerful spirit consume my senses and the room felt as though it were filled with light. My heart felt as though it might leap from my chest. We both sat quiet for a few moments recognizing the emotion in the room. I finally dared myself to speak.

"Servie, if God has asked you – to ask me – to write your book, then the answer is – yes," I cried.

Servie buried her face in her hands and wept. What courage

it must have taken to ask. She felt a mix of gratitude and elation. I immediately knew that I should accept this calling, but also felt completely overwhelmed at the idea. I didn't even know her story yet. My head screamed *no*, but my heart screamed *yes*. I shook my head in disbelief at what I had just committed myself to.

"Servie, did you ask me because you knew that I had written a book?" I said.

Her eyes widened.

"You mean you wrote a book?" Servie said.

Unbelievable. This woman I barely knew had just asked me to write her life story and didn't even know that I could put a sentence together. There was no doubt God's hand was in this.

I ran out to my car and grabbed a copy of my book. "Please read some of this Servie," I said. "I want you to see my style of writing. See if it is right for you."

Servie thanked me for the book and thumbed through its pages.

"I will read it," Servie said. "But I don't need to know from your book. God has told me that it is right."

What incredible faith this woman has. I was immediately impressed by her courage and clear belief that she was guided.

I cried all the way home. I understood the hard work ahead of me. It felt impossible. But I also knew that God was behind this request. I needed the same strong faith that Servie had in me. And I knew that I would have to get down on my knees to find it.

There have been hours and hours of taped interviews with Servie. Slowly her story came out. I love this woman. We have laughed together and cried together. She had to visit painful memories in order to help me feel her story. There was not a chapter written that I didn't shed tears as my fingers typed the words. Yes, I feel this story.

Servie wants her story to be told, but she also wants to teach. She has learned valuable lessons in her life and wants to share that with others. It is a book which gives a glimpse into her tragedies and her triumphs. And it is a book which enlightens and inspires.

What have I learned? Everyone has a story. If we can find God and pull his influence into our stories, then we can do hard things. Each of our stories are different, but our spirits reach for His light. Our hearts are one in purpose, or as Servie would say:

"We all sing the same song."

INTRODUCTION

Our eyes were wide with anticipation. As the road took another bend we eagerly peered out the car windows – stretching our necks to catch the first glimpse.

We were surrounded by beauty. Tall majestic mountains filled with lush greenery. Brilliant blue water – a reflection of the sky above. It was exhilarating. But the immediate surroundings in Germany were secondary to the destination. Just a bit further …

Then suddenly it came into view. We gasped, then fell silent. A sight which somehow was the perfect depiction of a fairy tale. That perfectly dreamy life. All eyes and emotions focused on the scene before us: The Neuschwanstein Castle.

Just seven weeks after the death of King Ludwig II in 1886, Neuschwanstein was opened to the public. The shy king had built the castle in order to withdraw from public life. Now vast numbers of tourists come to view his private refuge. Neuschwanstein is one of the most popular of all the palaces and castles in Europe. Every year over 1.4 million people visit this castle of the fairy tale king.[1] It is a magical imagery of fairy tales read to us as children and retold decades later to our own. The Neuschwanstein Castle is a striking vision of a fantasy life where dreams really do come true.

We all grow up wanting the fairy tale. As adults, we secretly wish for it. The fairy tale that the world shows us is smooth, easy, beautiful. Songs are upbeat and flow with exciting melodies. Life in the world's fairy tale is effortless. It is predictable. It is about receiving – not giving. The mortal, tired and fearful part of us wants that fairy tale. We yearn for it – particularly when challenges pull us down. Our real-life songs are sometimes dark, emotional and melancholy. So, we desperately dream and set our hearts on reaching for that fairy tale.

And, why wouldn't we? Movie productions make millions displaying it on the big screen and it starts when we are young. Beautiful and exciting and colorful characters singing happy songs. Festivities and dancing on cobblestone streets lined with colorful dwellings and flowers in window sills. Hurt feelings between characters are resolved in minutes. We grow up loving this make-believe life on the screen in our homes, in theaters and on the stage. Yes – we want that fairy tale. We want our life to be one big beautiful melody that plays in fields of sunflowers and sunshine. But it is not what we signed up for. In fact, we voted against it.

We signed up for something much bigger. And better. So much better. Each life would be a story. It would be a story of great difficulty. A story of happiness. A story of gut-wrenching decisions. A story of joy. A story of despair. A story of peace. A story of heartache. A story of miracles. Tears. Laughter. All wrapped into one big book whose chapters symbolize life. Our life.

The chapters won't define us. But they will shape us. Change us. Expand and refine our soul. We signed up to live each chapter in this story of our life because of how it ends. The happily ever after in this story is better than any fairy tale shown on the big screen. It is the incredible promise of becoming more like God. Gaining His understanding for ourselves because we've lived and felt. And it is returning to live with Him again in a world more glorious than we can even imagine. That is the true fairy tale.

What is the story of your book? It is different for each one of us. There are both hills and valleys on our journey. Despite what is put in front of us, it is once again looking for Him. It is searching for the eternal happily ever after. Sometimes we get a glimpse. And other times it seems so very far away.

Once upon a time there was a woman with a beautiful soul and a tender heart. This is her story, and this is her song.

CHAPTER 1

Shattered Dreams

"The greatest battle of life is fought out within the silent chambers of your own soul."
David O. McKay

Servie felt a single tear trickle down her cheek. And she let it fall. A few tears were allowed, but the waterfall of emotion that was fighting for release must not surface. She must hold it together – for Kimberly. The enormity of what she was about to do consumed her senses. It defied all logic. It fought against her motherly instinct. And it was breaking her heart.

Servie heard the final call. A blaring announcement at the airport gate that boarding would soon begin. She took a deep breath and exhaled slowly trying to calm her racing heart and restless stomach. Servie dared herself to look back one more time. A final glance at the 2-year-old daughter she was walking away from. How could she leave her? So young and impressionable. Little Kimberly would be old enough to know that her mother was missing. Yet young enough to not understand why.

It was unthinkable. But Servie knew it as her only choice. Her mother-heart fought against reason. Two realities battling against each other. To hold and to love her children. And to provide for their future. She could not do both in Zimbabwe.

Servie's thoughts took her back a few years to happier times, like the day she noticed him at church. Stealing glances between sermons. She had just finished high school. So young, but so in love. Soon the courtship with the kind young man from church turned into a beautiful marriage. A partnership with a husband who worked hard at a bookkeeping job to support five beautiful children that they were blessed with. His investment was theirs. Hard work which would materialize into future dreams for this family. She managed all the activities and routines necessary for their upbringing: loving and nurturing children, teaching them the value of hard work, and providing a place where souls are shaped and hearts are touched and softened.

It was a happy little place in a tiny village called Mtshabezi. A village where your neighbors sat together in worship at church. Most houses were constructed of wood and mud topped with thatched roofs. Two small windows allowed for light during the day and a wick lamp for evening. Water was hauled into the homes. Many had dirt floors. Children ran freely through village roads and were doted on by all. It was simple. It was beautiful. And it was home.

Nobody ever said Servie didn't give her all. She was a daughter, a mother and a friend who worked sunup to sundown giving everything to others. Formal education beyond high school in her own life had not been a priority. Helping her mother and caring for others was paramount. Her life was a mission of serving others. But she wanted more for her children. More than she ever had. She knew some measure of their future success hinged on formal education. And she was determined to provide that opportunity for all her children. Servie would make sure they had a fighting chance.

Servie and her husband had the foresight to set these children on a path of education, a path that would surely lead to freedom and opportunity outside of this tiny village in Zimbabwe. The country was deteriorating quickly and work was scarce. Education opened doors. They knew that and worked hard scraping and saving to make sure each child walked through that gateway.

Just over two years ago, her family was on track. Each child growing up and working hard to accomplish goals their parents had set for them. Hopes and dreams for these children were becoming a reality.

Thabani was her oldest son. A quiet, beautiful boy. Never a quarrel or fight with anyone. Not even the neighborhood bullies. His name means "happiness." A fitting and appropriate name describing both this child and the mood of this beautiful little household. Thabani was a humble soul who was always obedient. After high school, he hoped to work in South Africa and study accounting – learn business skills in a college far away from this tiny village. He wanted to be the first to open the exit door and walk out of Zimbabwe and into a brighter future; he wanted to make his parents proud. An uncle there in South Africa had offered his home until Thabani could provide for himself. Servie and her husband dreamed of his future success. Hopes that he would one day own his own business. Two parents whose dream was their son's prosperity. She could see the vision.

Then came Thembelani. A second child whose name captured the feelings of this happy couple's growing family. His name means "we have hope." A handsome little brother known for his intelligence at such a young age. In church one day the preacher asked everybody to stand up who had memorized five Bible verses. Thembelani stood as tall as his young frame allowed.

He marched himself up to the front. The preacher asked, "What is the shortest verse in the Bible?"

"Jesus wept," he proudly exclaimed. The congregation cheered.

Thembelani went on to high school to be named Math Olympiad. He was the number one math student in Zimbabwe. An achievement which made his parents proud. After high school, he jumped at the opportunity to study actuarial science in college. There were good colleges in the UK and relatives were there to support him.

Thandeka was a beautiful little girl who had a big heart and a strong desire to serve her family. Whenever she wasn't studying, she was always the first to care for the younger children. Her name, which means "lovable," perfectly described this child full of charity. Servie depended on Thandeka for help with the laundry, cooking and bathing duties. As a young teenager, she grabbed an opportunity to attend high school in the UK. Servie's sister was living there and the schools in Zimbabwe were declining rapidly, so Thandeka left to pursue a higher education abroad in a boarding school. She had seen older siblings embark on a strong future and with the urging of her parents, she followed along the path they had set.

Thembelihle was a happy little sister who always made good decisions and had a solid respect for elders. During her high school years, she would attend a boarding school in Zimbabwe. A simple setup offering scholastic opportunities for children at a small cost. It was a better option than the village school where teachers may or may not show up for the day. Servie's sister worked at the boarding school and made assurances that she would watch over this little girl. Thembelihle watched her brothers and sisters study hard and understood the sacrifice her parents were making for all their futures. Thembelihle means "good hope." A middle child who understood family values and valiant efforts. She believed her future was bright.

Mlungisi was the youngest brother. A funny little boy with a big sense of humor and a love of all sports. Three times in elementary school he won Sportsman of the Year award. Soccer was his favorite sport. A playful boy who never stopped running and made everyone smile – especially his mother. A good boy who wanted to please.

His name means "someone who makes things right." Yes, indeed he tried. An appropriate and fitting name for this littlest brother.

"Off you go," his mother would wave. "Go keep an eye on your sisters."

He walked behind them just far enough to be out of sight. Darting in and out when they would turn around. A silly game of hide and seek. Choosing to do what his mother had asked and having fun in the process.

And then a final pregnancy. A sixth child to soon bless this marriage of 20 years. Servie considered her treasures. Five beautiful souls who were born and raised by two loving parents. A family living in simple circumstances, but rich in love. The movement in her belly made her smile. This little one had spunk. Perhaps eager to join the others.

But this fairy tale would suddenly shatter. A chapter in Servie's story nobody predicted. A chapter which would alter the entire course of her life.

Three months into the pregnancy "happily ever after" was violently snatched from Servie's life. It was a tragic car accident that took the life of her husband. A single, devastating moment which changed everything and left her alone to support five souls with another on the way. A vicious and abrupt end to a 20-year marriage. A horrific end to a beautiful union. One single unexplainable moment that became a chapter which would force a new direction. A path of emptiness, loneliness and pain that is felt deep in the soul.

Friends and family gathered for his funeral. Together they cried and pulled each other close in support over what looked like a collapse of this family's future. What would this mean for them? Servie felt numb with grief and disbelief. Others would hold her up. Concern for her health and welfare was foremost in everyone's mind. How would she do this?

Weeks of grief turned into months. Each day Servie rose with the sun and willed herself to climb out of bed, the pillow on the other side of the bed still neatly positioned consuming Servie with despair. Her heart ached. The darkness penetrated her soul and begged to overtake her senses. She shook her head as if to remove the thought. Just get through the day …

Five months later Servie recognized the familiar pains. But, oh – it was much too early. Labor pains twisted like a giant rubber band around her middle, then wrapped around to her back. The pain caused her to catch her breath. There was no stopping this one.

Servie closed her eyes and took a deep breath. How would she do this alone? This child would never know her father. The pain in her heart was heavy. It fought to consume her, but was interrupted by another racking pain. The intensity of labor told her it was time.

Servie was rushed to the hospital. Doctors monitored the situation. Servie's blood pressure was much too high. A quick decision was made. This baby would need to be removed immediately.

With limited knowledge and equipment in a small hospital in Zimbabwe, doctors did their best to save baby and mother. A large vertical incision was made. A violent opening from top to bottom of Servie's burgeoning belly. An entrance into a harsh new world for this little one. A place where joy once lived was now a place of hardship. A place of disheartenment. A world of hurt.

The hospital staff gently placed the baby in Servie's arms. An immediate love for this child consumed Servie's broken heart. Somehow a piece of her husband's soul had come to life. A beautiful reminder of what once was. A glimpse of hope.

Servie gently kissed the delicate features. A tiny, beautiful little girl. So tiny that Servie wondered if this child would live. But this little one would fight. A strong spirit who would surely influence the lives of so many. Servie named her Kimberly Bongwe. In the Zulu language of Africa Bongwe means "thank you, Lord." Gratitude for a gift recognized by a grieving mother.

Caring for this little tiny gift at home was draining. Servie pushed hard on her breast to express the milk. This tiny little baby could not suck. And so around the clock Servie would fill a teaspoon and carefully pour it into Kimberly's mouth. A necessary feeding regiment to give her a chance. This little one barely cried. Just a faint squeaking sound. So small and fragile.

Week after week the caring continued. Kimberly was responding well, but still so tiny. Servie didn't dare take her out into public. She kept her wrapped and covered.

Servie quietly placed Kimberly in her bed. The youngest boy Mlungisi had finished his schoolwork and was fast asleep next to sweet Thembelihle. The three older children were away at school.

Darkness. The stars acting as a nightlight in the Zimbabwe sky. Finally, her house was quiet. She had done it. Survived one more day.

Servie's head hit the pillow. She pulled the covers up under her chin. Tucked them tight around her face. The worry was beginning to consume her. Financially it was becoming increasingly difficult. There just wasn't enough. The enormity of her situation was closing in. She took the blanket in her hands and dabbed her cheeks. Wiping away streams of discouragement and hopelessness.

"No time for tears," she whispered to herself. Six children were depending on her. Thabani, Thembelani, Thandeka, Thembelihle, Mlungisi and tiny Kimberly. Somehow … she must wake the next morning and find a way.

Servie was up with the sun. She ran out to the garden in the back of the house. Surveyed what was left. Once a garden bursting with cabbage, carrots, peas, beans, tomatoes and spinach. Sugarcane, watermelon and white pumpkins were a special treat. But now the crop was nearly exhausted. She could perhaps stretch it a bit further. "I'll go without," she thought. "More for the children." She carefully watered the remaining plants.

Neighbors and family helped out. Milk for the baby needed to be purchased each Sunday. Some weeks there wasn't enough money. Food and milk money was donated and service rendered to care for her children. It was helpful and Servie recognized the love. But this could not go on forever. She must find another way.

Ten-hour bus trips were taken to Botswana. Clothing was purchased there with a handful of money given to her by family. She could buy clothing cheaper there and sell for a profit back home. But there was a risk. The border officers in Botswana didn't approve of the visits. Servie frequently found a quiet corner under a porch to spend the night before boarding a bus the next morning. The officers often beat the Zimbabwe citizens. Servie recalled one night when she was hit by an officer's fist so hard on her face that she was certain she had lost her eye. She would return to Zimbabwe the following day with clothing bundled up. Back on the streets in Zimbabwe she was desperate to sell the items. Some days were good. Most were not.

Servie counted the money she kept in the drawer. She counted again and shook her head. There was not enough for a bus fare today. Thembelihle and Mlungisi would have to stay home from school. Education was becoming a hardship along with everything else.

Servie thought back to the visit from her sister who had moved away to New York City. She came to Zimbabwe for a visit to check on her sister and to present a plan.

"Come live with me for a bit. I'll purchase your airline ticket. I'll help you find work. Leave the children here. It's only temporary. You can send money back to help feed the children and pay for their schooling. There is no work in Zimbabwe. This is a way out."

Servie's sister begged her to think about it. Family members would pull money together to keep the children in their schools while things got settled. Servie's brother lived in the same village of Mtshabezi. He and his wife could care for her younger children – raise Kimberly as their own for a bit. Watch over the other children.

Emotionally it sounded impossible. But her heart pounded as she considered the thought. Something telling her that it was right. Perhaps God knew her circumstance and was opening a door. A door which felt impossible to walk through. But, perhaps, a door which led to hope.

Servie wiped away evidence of the few tears which couldn't be held back. Her heart beat so loudly that she could hear it inside her head. She wondered if anyone here at the airport could as well. She allowed herself an anguished glance back toward her family.

The announcement for last boarding blared throughout the airport. The words felt like a slug in the stomach. Servie shook her head bringing herself back to the present – January 2000. Back to reality. She looked down at her feet. Willing them to take a step. They felt like lead blocks. Was there any other choice? She had gone over and over the options in her mind. Felt the pain of it in her heart. But she knew this was the only way. A plan of desperation. A heart-wrenching sacrifice. She knew she must do this. She must surrender to the plan for her children.

And so Servie turned and took the longest walk of her life. Through the gate and up the ramp to the aircraft. This ride would take her away from Zimbabwe, Africa, to a foreign land over 7,000 miles away. Halfway around the world from the only place she had ever known. Halfway around the world from a tiny village where neighbors were like family. Halfway around the world from her six children. And halfway around the world from a wide-eyed toddler who loved and needed her mother.

CHAPTER 2

Divine Nature

*"Live so that those who know you and don't know Him
will want to know Him because they know you."*
Unknown

Servie hurried home from school. She knew that her mom needed help with the little ones. There was work around the house and gardens to tend. Babies needed to be bathed and fed. So much to do. As the oldest of eight children, Servie understood what it took to keep a busy household running. And she understood her part in it.

She counted the streets as she skipped home, looking down each street as she passed. Each house familiar. This little village was her world.

School mornings were especially busy. Just getting everybody out the door was a feat. Servie felt a sense of satisfaction. She was an essential part of this big family, and she loved her part in helping Mom and Dad with this happy brood of youngsters.

But today was Friday. A fabulous day which signaled the end of the school week. Servie loved weekends spent playing and working together as a family. It was a connection to something bigger. Something bigger than their little modest home. Something bigger than this family unit.

Sundays were spent in church. Mom and dad made that a priority. Friends and family gathering under a small roof to pay respect to God. It was a 5-mile walk to the Christian church building. The children knew that Mom would let them pick berries from the trees and eat them on the long walk home. A tasty treat after worship.

Servie considered her limited understanding. She believed that God was real. And she was taught that he heard prayers – though she had never uttered one herself. She supposed you had to learn a lot more before you could address Him personally. But she felt sure that He was there. Her heart told her so.

The preacher read from the Bible, "*All things were made by him …*" (John 1:3).

Servie contemplated what that might mean.

. . .

Let's consider the concept that God created us. What if we reflected on that every morning as we rose to greet another day? If we come from God, then we should assume that we have threads of divinity within us. A divine nature.

There are over 7 billion people on the earth. That's a lot of differences. Different colors, different cultures and different attributes. But with all our differences, there is a powerful thread which connects us. One not seen, but very real. A thread of divinity. A brilliant light in each of us that aligns us with Him.

No one was ever quite like you. The Lord made only one, without carbons. You are not repeated and not repeatable. No one else can do what the Lord sent you to mortality to do. The value of what you have to contribute will come through the expression of your own personality – that particular spark of the divine that makes you unique. It sets you off from every other living creature. The mark you leave on the world is as individual as you. The difference you make and the mark you leave on the hearts and minds of others is as distinct as your thumbprint.

It is a source of goodness within. A spiritual property that we are born with. Perhaps that is why we stare in wonder at a newborn baby. A miraculous bundle of purity and worth. Our spirit recognizing something. Something bigger than us. Something divine.

· · ·

Servie would be graduating from high school soon. She pondered what her future might be. Perhaps a big important job. College in one of those fancy universities. She had read in school about opportunities outside her simple neighborhood. Hope for a better future. Perhaps she could be a teacher. Own a business. She allowed herself to imagine a glimpse of something bright and exciting. Something important. She wanted to make a difference.

"Servie! Come quickly and help your sister," yelled her mother in a stern, yet loving voice.

Servie brought her attention back to the present. No time for those dreams. Her mom needed help and her younger siblings depended on her. Earlier that year, a terrible accident had taken the life of their father. A fateful, heartbreaking event that changed the order of things. Mother was now the head of this household, and Servie knew it was her obligation to help. As the oldest sister, she would try to fill the empty spot.

After helping with the younger children and gathering fresh

vegetables from the garden, Servie leaned back in her chair. The front porch was her favorite spot. A place where she could keep a close eye on the children and shout a friendly "hello" to neighbors. The stew was simmering in a pot, the smell penetrating the house and finding its way out onto the porch. Dinner would be ready soon.

Her younger sister jumped and twirled around. Servie laughed at the display. Perhaps this little one was a future dancer. She certainly had the energy.

Suddenly she heard them. The roar of engines. Servie's eyes darted back and forth trying to locate each of the children. The cars. They were coming.

"Hurry!" she screamed. "Everybody inside!"

It was happening again. A more regular occurrence. Cars of white people racing through their village. White people looking to kill black people.

Servie's mother put her finger to her lips. The children sensed the danger – the threat of being discovered. They huddled together in her protective embrace.

How long would this continue? The villagers were shaken. Recently the white people were questioning anybody they saw on the street.

"Who do you support?" they screamed.

People mumbled whatever they thought the white people wanted to hear. Sometimes it was acceptable. Other times the white people suspected dishonesty. Immediate death was the fateful consequence.

For weeks Servie and her mother took turns sleeping. Nights were long and frightening. Sleep was secondary to safety. For Zimbabwe, apartheid had become a very real and tragic part of the regime. And the small villages suffered greatly.

Men with guns terrified the people. Some soldiers were there to kill. Others attempted to organize or gather information. The villagers didn't know who to trust.

"I want you to kill that chicken and cook it for me," they demanded. Then they would leave with the owner's cow, often leaving a family financially devastated. Many kept all their money in their homes. Life savings taken in one terrible minute. But it got worse.

"Today your wife is going to be my wife," the men would boast. Women and families emotionally and physically tortured. The stories were widespread and shared to warn other villagers. But Servie's family knew firsthand about the assaults. Her aunt and uncle had recently been attacked. They had not seen them coming before it was too late. A group of evil men broke through the front door. One noticed their daughter.

"This girl is mine today," he snarled. The others held the father and mother and forced them to watch as her innocence was snatched away in a brutal act of rape. Then they built a campfire and made the mother sit on it. They wanted to burn her alive. Fortunately, she survived. It was a horrific reality of the times.

The murders and the violence continued to the point that everyone in the village had to leave: homes they had built, large vegetable gardens which fed families, a lifetime of hard work in building a community where families could live, learn and love. They had heard about a neighboring village. The men had killed everybody and buried them in a single grave. Would they be next?

Servie's mother said there was no choice. It was simply too dangerous to stay. And they must all stick together.

Servie tried not to think about it. Their lives were most

important. She helped her mother grab the bare necessities. They must leave with their friends and flee together. They had heard there was greater safety in a town 60 kilometers away. Families could group together and find shelter in a few single-room huts. It was the best chance for survival.

The plan was to leave at midnight. It would take a couple of days to walk there. Servie helped her mother with the children. They would carry their basic belongings on top of their heads and take turns carrying the baby. Water would be located along the way.

Servie turned and took a final look. A quick glance at the street. Her home. That beautiful front porch. She promised herself they would return.

The little family walked all night and most of the following day. Upon arrival in the town, they found a small place to call home. Everyone collapsed. Hunger pains were secondary to exhaustion. For now, they were safe. They curled up together on the floor and slept.

The following morning a sunrise declared the beginning of a new day. Servie's mother reminded the children that God was looking after them. Living conditions were tough, but they had each other. And they had God. Mother gathered them together in prayer each day in their small, primitive living space. This little family would cling together in one room and learn how to survive. Work was scarce and unprofitable. They sold everything they could do without. Everything had to be bought and sold or traded. There was no room for large vegetable gardens. Those were a distant memory.

Sometimes at night Servie would close her eyes and think back to their garden. Remember the taste of fresh grown vegetables and sweet melons. How they felt in her hands as she tended them.

The smell. They were so missed. How many days could they survive on just bread? Perhaps tomorrow there would be something better...

Servie felt her mother's hand on her arm. She awakened and looked to her mother for direction. Then she heard it. Shouting and hollering. Babies crying. Another gathering. Her heart raced and she felt a pit in her stomach.

Servie collected her siblings and moved them along. Mom cradled the baby in her arms. Everyone was tired. It was dark. What time was it? Did that really matter? Servie's tired body told her it was the middle of the night. As they walked outside, Servie looked up at the moon – grateful for the light it provided as they marched. It was yet another dreaded riot. And attendance was not optional.

As the crowd gathered the leaders shouted off commands. War songs. How Servie hated this required duty. There was no choice. And it was happening with increased frequency. Shouting and banging on doors in the middle of the night. You leave everything, grab the children and come together to show allegiance.

It was frightening. It was exhausting. If only her father were here. Servie's heart longed for his leadership, for the strength he was to the family and for his love.

. . .

South Africa's people represent a kaleidoscope of cultures. The first people to live in southern Africa were the Khoikhoi and the San. These brown-skinned herders and hunters were eventually joined by darker-skinned groups migrating from central Africa into the fertile western valleys of southern Africa. In the seventeenth century, several European cultures moved in and adopted it as their homeland. In the late eighteenth century, the British came with a number of servants from India and Asia.

Having lived separately for hundreds of years, these cultures were now compressed together. South Africa is unique in that a wide variety of cultures were mixed together in a short period of time and in a small space. Apartheid was based on the philosophy that separate peoples should pursue their own cultural and economic paths.[1]

Pulling these different cultures together is no easy task. Difficult challenges are certain. Even today we identify ourselves in many different ways, including our place of birth, our nationality and our language. Some identify themselves by their occupation or their hobby. The earthly identities that we categorize ourselves into are not wrong unless they supersede or interfere with our eternal identity – that of being a son or a daughter of God.

This doctrine is so basic and so beautifully simple that it can seem ordinary. In reality, it is among the most extraordinary knowledge we can obtain. An understanding of who we really are. That in itself could have a powerful influence on how we treat and respect one another.[2] We do what we know. Knowledge is paramount. It changes lives. One life at a time, we can change the world.

. . .

Servie helped the children gather up their belongings.

"Come now!" she urged. "We're going home! Let's work together."

It had been five long years living like refugees in a room they called home. An agreement was made and the government said it was now safe to return to their villages. Oh, the thought of it! She wondered what had become of their home. Rumors had surfaced that everything in the villages had been either stolen or destroyed. The thought of it made her weep. But the longing to return home had now become a reality. They would restart.

After miles of travel they were finally on the outskirts of their village. Servie grabbed her mother's hand. She mentally steeled herself for what she was about to see. Just another street or two.

Their eyes darted back and forth trying to take it all in. Any hope of finding what they had left was gone. Their hearts broken by the vision. Homes completely ransacked. Any remaining possessions were broken and strewn everywhere. It was a wave of destruction. Their beautiful village was almost unrecognizable.

The little family turned the corner toward home. Servie took a deep breath before she would allow herself to see. To feel. Oh, that beautiful front porch. The memory of it so real. It had kept her going for the last five years. She lifted her head.

It was worse than they had imagined. Only one wall of the house remained. The roof was gone. Everything once a part of this simple, loving home was broken. Wood and furniture scattered about. Their garden was gone. The little family held each other and wept. Tears of despair at the sight. Tears of weariness from years of hiding in fear. But also tears of gratitude. They had each other. And they would start over from the ground up.

"God will help us," Servie's mother said. "Come together now. Let us pray."

And so they all worked together. Everyone in the village helped each other as homes were built and gardens were planted. One day at a time. Success was small. But they could see the vision.

Normalcy was on the horizon.

Servie traveled to Botswana buying clothing and other small goods. She knew a good deal when she saw one and knew what could be sold in Zimbabwe for a profit. Servie was eager to help her mother support the family. After months of hard work, she finally had enough money to purchase five cows for the family. They would have milk. What a blessing!

Bottles were filled and marked for sale. Mother decided on five cents.

"Servie – fill those bottles and take them to all the neighbors' homes to sell. Five cents a bottle. A fair price. Hurry along now."

Mother knew that these cows could provide for her family and also bring a source of income.

Servie ran to each home. It was wonderful to see everyone. Hugs and kisses. A light breeze filled the air. Years of anguish were quietly and slowly ushering in a new season. One of hope.

After hours of visiting she turned back toward home. Walked up the steps onto the porch and met her mother's gaze.

Servie had returned with no milk – and no money.

"Mom, I can't sell the milk. We need to help them."

Servie had given away everything. One of the other children would need to handle this task.

Mother shook her head. Oh this child … such a tender, loving soul.

. . .

The story of our search for happiness is written in such a way that if we do good things and continue to trust in God through the challenging times, even those times will bring us closer to the happiness we are seeking. Children are usually good examples of happy, giving hearts and a cheerful countenance. They possess a sense of happiness and optimism that invites others to rejoice with them.[3]

In 2 Corinthians 9:7 we read, *"Every man according as he purposeth in his heart, so let him give; not grudgingly, or of necessity: for God loveth a cheerful giver."*

Often it is the children who show us the way. Their young hearts see the world in a simpler way. Without distraction and complicated agendas, they see the better way. His way.

Usually we measure "rich" and "poor" from the perspective of temporal possessions, but there are other ways to be both rich and poor – other ways to consider and measure. We can certainly learn gratitude for knowing who we are and for a chance to help someone else know more about who they are – especially with regard to their relationship to God and their purpose for being on this earth. That knowledge is crucial and changes our focus from challenging current situations to one of hope as we consider eternal goals.

We are children of our Heavenly Father. When we lived with Him during our experience in premortality, we were taught by Him about a beautiful plan which involved coming to earth to learn, to feel and to experience an opportunity to grow. We not only voted for that opportunity – we cheered.[4] *"When the morning stars sang together, and all the sons of God shouted for joy ..."* (Job 38:7).

In our premortal state we were among the sons and daughters of God who shouted for joy because of the opportunity to come to this challenging yet necessary mortal existence. We understood and knew that our purpose was to gain a physical body, to overcome trials, and to prove that we would keep the commandments of God.[5] We understood that a veil would be drawn over our memories so that we would be free either to walk by faith and by the Spirit or to forsake our spiritual heritage and birthright.

Now we are here. It is a time of testing, and a time of probation. Will we keep the proper focus? We would all agree that challenges and responsibilities, at times, seem to overshadow almost everything else. But there is power in knowledge. Studying and working toward a fuller understanding of a plan that is a crucial part of our divinity.

We have such an influence and an ability to enrich all of humanity. There is divine potential in each of us. With that divinity come innate gifts, blessings, and endowments. As we recognize that potential we have more trust in the Lord and more hope in His word. This inner spiritual sense gives us a certain resilience to cope with sorrow, trouble and uncertainty.[6]

We know that the ultimate goal is eternal life and to return to our divinity having learned a thing or two from our mortal experience. Elder Dallin H. Oaks explained: "*The Final judgment is not just an evaluation of a sum total of good and evil acts – what we have done. It is an acknowledgment of the final effect of our acts and thoughts – what we have become. It is not enough for anyone just to go through the motions. The commandments, ordinances, and covenants of the gospel are not a list of deposits required to be made in some heavenly account. The gospel of Jesus Christ is a plan that shows us how to become what our Heavenly Father desires us to become.*"[7]

In "becoming" we influence others. And they notice. In John 8:12 we read, "*I am the light of the world: he that followeth me shall not walk in darkness, but shall have the light of life.*"

Have you ever been in total darkness? Turned your flashlight off when inside a cave? We are grateful when the light flows in after such moments.

Helen Keller was a person who made her way through this world in that kind of darkness, and yet she found light in her darkness. She held a strong sense of her identity and the divine nature of the human soul. She said, *"Truly, I have looked into the very heart of darkness and refused to yield to its paralyzing influence, but in spirit I am one of those who walk in the morning."*[8]

It is our destiny to choose and embrace and rejoice in our wonderful identity and the power that will flow as we, too, walk in the morning and bring the bright light to this dark world. The power of our example will move the work of our Father forward. He reminds us,

"Ye are the light of the world. A city that is set on a hill cannot be hid. Neither do men light a candle, and put it under a bushel, but on a candlestick; and it giveth light unto all that are in the house. Let your light so shine before men, that they may see your good works, and glorify your Father which is in Heaven" (Matthew 5:14-16).[9]

The aspiration and the aim is ours. To live up to the great and magnificent inheritance which the Lord God, our Father in Heaven, has provided for us. To rise above the dust of the world. To know that we are children with a divine birthright. To walk in the sun with our heads high – knowing that we are loved and honored, that we are a part of His kingdom, and that there is for us a great work to be done which cannot be left to others.[10]

CHAPTER 3

Live Your Truth

*"… Be strong and of a good courage; be not afraid,
neither be thou dismayed: for the Lord thy God is with
thee whithersoever thou goest."*

Joshua 1:9

The flight was unbelievably long. Every hour an agonizing reminder of the growing distance between Servie and her children. Her eyes were swollen from raw emotion that spilled over for hours. And the throbbing in her head kept pace with her pounding heart.

"Let's just get there," she thought.

As if a private conversation were occurring with the pilot, he suddenly announced over the intercom that the descent into New York City had begun. Servie put the tray table back into place and took a mental inventory of her belongings. She had checked a small suitcase containing gifts for her sister. Above her in the overhead compartment was a small bag holding a few clothes and one sweater.

She felt a surge of anxiety. She had seen pictures of the big cities. They didn't seem real. All that cement and metal. The thought of it was suffocating.

Servie leaned over to get a glimpse out the airplane window.

Everything was white. It was January and clearly there had been a snowstorm. Her sister told her to wear warm clothes. January in Zimbabwe averages 80 degrees. So Servie put on a simple dress and high heels. The perfect outfit for attending church on a beautiful winter day back home. She smoothed the wrinkles in the skirt and watched the white flakes hit the window.

The airplane gradually began its final descent dropping closer and closer to the big city. Every minute this crazy plan felt closer to reality. Servie took a deep breath and tried to quiet her racing heart. She averted her eyes away from the gray and white scene below. It was closing in much too fast. She closed her eyes and braced herself for contact, for a new world – a world without her children.

Servie exited the plane and followed the crowd to the baggage area. She looked at the people racing through the airport. Eyes of steel focused on getting somewhere. Faces displaying no emotion. Feet dashing here and there. What was this awful place? Her sister should be here to meet her any minute. She turned to look for her.

That's when she noticed that all eyes were on her. Everybody was wearing long coats and winter boots. She looked down at her silk dress and high heels. A favorite outfit of hers. Suddenly she felt unprepared and out of place. It felt as though she had landed on another planet.

Servie grabbed her luggage and walked toward the airport doors. Through the glass she could see taxi cabs and buses sweeping through the area. The blast of cold air took her breath away when the doors opened. She had never felt that kind of cold.

She tucked her head into her shoulders as the wind whipped through her dress. Snowflakes flew into her face. So, this was snow. She felt the flakes flutter across her nose. Servie had always seen pictures. It looked so gentle in magazines and in movies. This was fierce. And so very cold.

Servie heard her name. She turned and saw her sister holding a large coat. She opened up the coat and motioned for Servie to come get warm.

Servie grabbed her suitcase and rushed toward family. But high heels and snow don't mix. The combination flung Servie up into the air and back down onto the snow-covered sidewalk. She felt a searing pain in her knee.

"Welcome to New York City," she thought.

Perhaps this was a mistake. Her sister rushed over, gathered Servie up into her arms and held her tight, helping her limp over to the car.

"Let's get you home and take a look at that knee."

Servie looked out the window as they drove through city streets. The buildings were taller than she had imagined from the airplane window. A sea of gray. Metal and cement in every direction. And so many people. It was stifling. Fear consumed her senses.

They pulled up to the apartment building. Where were the gardens? There was nothing green in sight. Where were the neighbors? The children? The porches?

Servie switched her attention from the pain in her knee to the pain in her heart. Thoughts went back to her own children. Her brother and sister-in-law would care for the younger children. Her mother would help on weekends. They would be cared for. But nobody could love them like Servie did. A mother's love is not replaceable. Her heart ached with grief.

Servie awoke to a knee swollen up to twice its normal size. Medical attention was required and surgery for a torn ligament ordered. This wasn't the plan. She needed to work. Her whole purpose was to earn money to send to the children. Her recovery was an unbearable delay to her mission.

"Hello?" Servie reached across the bed and answered her cellphone. She knew from the number it was a call from Zimbabwe. She felt her stomach drop.

It was her brother. "Servie, we need money for milk. We need milk for Kimberly. We are getting low."

Servie's chin dropped to her chest. Her shoulders began to shake as she sobbed. She would have to ask other family members to help – again.

Servie's spirit began to spiral. Time was necessary to recover from surgery. Time would ensure that her knee could become strong again. But time became the enemy. Half a world away from her children, Servie sat and wondered. *Are the children happy? What are they doing right now? Do they miss me?* The combination of idle time and a broken heart began to take its toll. And Servie sunk into a deep depression.

The family rallied around her. Perhaps the big city was too much. Phone calls were made to some family in Indiana. A cousin spoke to Servie on the phone.

"Come live here and we'll help you find a job," he said. "It's a two-day bus ride. Live with us and we'll help you get settled."

Servie considered the rescue. A smaller city in Indiana. Maybe that would work. Her emotions were all over the place: one minute she was determined to return back home, gather her children and attempt to live off the land. And yet – a resolve to see this plan through. She must somehow find work and send money to provide food and an education for her little family. Perhaps they would one day come to the United States to live with her.

She remembered back to that original thought. A clear, unmistakable thought to come to the United States and secure a better life for her children. She knew it was right. But, oh, so much harder than she'd ever imagined.

"Okay, I'll get on the bus," she whispered.

Servie took a deep breath and closed her eyes tight, finding a thread of strength to move forward. It was a necessary plan. It was the plan. It was *her* plan. Servie's heart told her so.

. . .

The plan of salvation is not a movie of sorts that requires viewing. We are here as spiritual beings living a very mortal life. There is a difference between watching events unfold on the screen and living them. We could have all assembled in a theater and viewed examples and stories of what life on this earth might be. But our Heavenly Father knew better. Understanding and knowledge are not the same as living and feeling. This plan must involve struggle. Hard decisions. And action. It is a method of learning with all our senses. Choices are emotional and consequences felt. It is the ultimate learning experience, the ultimate refining process and the ultimate process allowing us to *become* something better.

Many of the modern Christian religions do not acknowledge that God makes any real demands on those who simply believe in Him, seeing Him rather as a butler who meets their needs or a therapist whose role is to help people feel good about themselves and their so-called authentic semblance.[1]

"By contrast," as one author declares, "the God portrayed in both the Hebrew and Christian Scriptures asks, not just for commitment, but for our very lives. The God of the Bible traffics in life and death, not niceness, and calls for sacrificial love, not benign whatever-ism."[2]

Remember that we each have divinity within us. That divine nature fuels a desire to serve others, follow our heart, and prompts us to take action. Even when that action seems impossibly hard.

Russell M. Nelson gave an emotional address to women: *"Today, let me add that we need women who know how to make important things happen by their faith and who are courageous defenders of morality and families in a sin-sick world. We need women who are devoted to shepherding God's children along the covenant path toward exaltation; women who know how to receive personal revelation, who understand the power and peace of the temple endowment; women who know how to call upon the powers of heaven to protect and strengthen children and families; women who teach fearlessly."*[3]

The divine nature within us propels us to move forward and to act on thoughts and desires that may feel monumental. But the whisperings of the Spirit within us speak to our soul. It is a method of communication. God knows our path and what is best. His communication to us comes through the Holy Ghost and is a transfer of thoughts, ideas and principles. This personal revelation helps us find our way in a dark and confusing world. It is a light on a dark path.

Julie B. Beck taught that *"the ability to qualify for, receive, and act on personal revelation is the single most important skill that can be acquired in this life. ... It requires a conscious effort."*[4] Notice the three steps:

- Qualify
- Receive
- Act

God knows our heart. He is aware of our righteous desires – desires which may seem beyond our ability to achieve. Often, we cannot see the way to bring about such an ambition. But God sees the big picture. And He knows when our mind and our heart is ready to receive. It is a whisper, a thought, a moment that causes us to stop and ponder. A fleeting moment that seems to pull all senses into one focus. It is so easily dismissed if we are not waiting and looking. But when recognized, it is powerful enough to consume our heart and mind for a time.

To act on personal revelation received can be the most difficult step. Especially if we are prompted to take a path that screams against our own plans. Our own tunnel vision prevents us from seeing how things could possibly work out. Sometimes when things are falling apart, they are actually falling into place. It is trusting the revelation that we receive and opening a door into unknown territory. A door where He knows what's waiting on the other side.

The more we practice these three steps of qualify, receive and act, the stronger our connection with God and the more we begin to trust Him. This personal revelation from the Spirit will prompt us to learn, speak and act on eternal truth – the Savior's truth. We do what we know because it is felt in the soul. The more we follow Christ, the more we will feel His love and direction. We are strengthened in our resolve to learn, speak, and act on His truth, even when we face opposition.

Our high responsibility is to follow the Savior, nurture with inspiration and live truth fearlessly. His power will flow into us as we act on personal revelation received to show us the way.[5] In a world of deception and lies and twisted paths, personal revelation is the only sure way to know the path. His path. A path which leads back to Him.

. . .

Servie heard a voice in her heart. Her tender heart was open and soft. She listened. It had felt like an impossible request. *"Go to the United States and find work to provide for your children."* She had wrestled with the idea, but ultimately took a blind step. With all the power within her soul and her mother's binding faith in God, Servie acted. She walked onto an airplane leaving behind six children. This was her truth. And she would live it fearlessly.

Servie peered out the bus window. She took a deep breath and exhaled slowly. It was the first time in weeks that she felt like she could breathe again. The landscape began to fill her empty soul with hope. Her eyes took it all in as the landscape whizzed by in a hurried blur. Gray had turned to green. And the metal had turned to moss. This seemed possible. There was much to accomplish, but just maybe, she could start.

Family rallied together and found employment possibilities in Indiana. They found a promising opportunity – a company which enabled people challenged by autism, intellectual and developmental disabilities, and related behavioral challenges to live more successful lives. There was a position open for an aide. No education or experience required. They were willing to train. Servie fiddled with the buttons on her blouse and nervously smoothed her hair. This interview might open a door. A way to earn some money. A way out. She squared her shoulders and walked into the office.

"Why yes," Servie answered, "I've cared for children my entire life."

Fortunately for Servie, the man across the desk saw her potential. And fortunately for this company, Servie would ride the bus every day and arrive to love and serve children in need. It was a way to fill the void. A way for her to give. It felt good to be needed. It was the perfect partnership. Her empty arms craved human touch. And these children craved acceptance and love. Children like Brian.

Brian was a 15-year-old boy who was severely autistic. He was one of her early assignments. Caring for a boy who could not care for himself. Servie fed him. Dressed him. Worked with him to learn simple skills. He hardly spoke. Brian lived in a world within his mind that was separate from our reality. His world could change from composure to violence in seconds. Servie understood that it was the autism that produced the outbursts. She held him tight and soothed. For months, she returned day after day to guide and assist.

One day Servie walked into work and heard her name.

"Miss Servie!"

She looked toward the voice. Her eyes darting back and forth to find the source.

"Miss Servie!" he said again. This time a tiny smile. And eyes filled with joy.

She looked at him in disbelief. Could it be? Brian had learned her name. She had only heard him utter groans and screams and nonsensical words. But this time he clearly stated her name. She threw her arms around him.

"Yes, Brian," she whispered. "I'm so happy to see you."

Servie volunteered to take as many hours as the company would give her. More hours meant more money. More money to send back to Zimbabwe for her children. More money to one day return home to visit. More money to one day pay a lawyer. Perhaps a lawyer could help her with papers to bring her children to the United States. A vision of these possibilities had once been blurry and distant, but now it seemed within focus. She let her co-workers know that she would cover all shifts for vacations and time off.

Her co-workers met together after work hours to go dancing. Evenings spent in bars and clubs. A celebration of friendship and a hard day's work. They encouraged Servie to join them. Servie politely declined. There was another place she'd rather be.

Servie had planted a small, modest vegetable garden at home. It became a refuge. A place that felt like home. The smell of the dirt. The feel of the vegetables in her hands. Cabbage, tomatoes, spinach, carrots – just like home. It was a connection to her village. And it was a connection to her children.

. . .

In 1 Corinthians 10:13, it says:

"There hath no temptation taken you but such as is common to man: but God is faithful, who will not suffer you to be tempted above that ye are able; but will with the temptation also make a way to escape, that ye may be able to bear it."

This is one of those scriptures that we embrace with fervor. It is a promise of hope and peace should we fall into the jaws of despair. And if we are in the midst of desperation and tribulation it is the safety net that we cling to with fingers clasped tight. It represents a light at the end of a tunnel. It represents unseen powers that are within our reach. And it represents a God who is aware with hands outstretched.

Neal A. Maxwell said: "... *the storm fronts that come into our lives will not last forever. We can surmount the drifts of difficulties and we can hold out if we maintain our perspective and faith. But while we are in the midst of all these things, the experiences that can be for our long-term good are very, very real. We may feel that such are simply more than we can bear. Yet if we have faith in an all-knowing and all-loving God, we understand He will not give us more than we can bear."[6]*

How often do we act on a prompting or personal revelation only to throw our hands up in discouragement because we feel abandoned and forgotten by God? We pray and tearfully ask, "Where are you," at our lowest point. We often dig deep pits for ourselves, then burn the escape ladder, but such irrationality is of our own willful doing – not God's.[7]

We are promised in the second half of 1 Corinthians 10:13 that He will "*also make a way to escape ...*" What does this mean? It means that life provides an opportunity for us to use our agency. That crucial promise which is essential to the plan of salvation. There will be testing for all of us – perhaps more for those who will walk in high places. Each individual is uniquely tested. But the greatest trials for many of us have to do with families, our congregation, our religion, our leaders, our country, and our friends. All things that have the potential of hurting us most.

Our souls are resilient. More than once, we find out how far we can bend and still not break. The Lord knows us better than we know ourselves. He is constantly molding us to the grand design of His great expectation and divine destiny. We will emerge through trial and testing as a more valued human soul. Each trial brings out the steel and velvet in us. Our commitment to the absolute truths of the gospel puts a steel in us that can endure tremendous pressure. On the other hand, the suffering brings about a velvet softness – a Christlike charity.[8]

If we are to emulate the lives of prophets in the scriptures or embrace and live principles taught, it requires more than an eternal perspective and a strong foundation. Knowledge is power when we understand the laws and the principles of Jesus Christ's gospel and the plan. But knowledge alone isn't enough to wade through a sea of sludge. Even years of experience and a strong testimony of His truths can sink when dashed hopes pull us down. To feel His outstretched arms, we need a solid dose of humility.

We read of Paul's devotion and humble service in the New Testament when he speaks of *"serving the Lord with all humility of mind, and with many tears, and temptations ..."* (Acts 20:19). If we don't serve the Lord with all humility, then we are really only serving ourselves.[9] The person with true humility will not seek to dignify or glorify himself. He will serve others for the sake of service. He will give his gifts in secret without boastful announcement. A humble heart realizes that all knowledge comes from God – for He knows all. A person with true humility will not be contentious, unruly, or critical. As a child of God, he will feel it a privilege to do His will and keep His commandments. A person with humility recognizes a partnership with God and the essential part He plays in directing us to do hard things.[10]

Paul understood this relationship. *"And now, behold, I go bound in the spirit unto Jerusalem, not knowing the things that shall befall me there ..."* (Acts 20:22). Paul is ready to take a leap of faith. A walk into the unknown. His mission is bigger than his life. His devotion is not inward. It is outward. He lived his truth. And he knew his truth was God's truth.

Dieter F. Uchtdorf promises:

"More than you could ever imagine, He wants you to achieve

your destiny – to return to your heavenly home in honor. I testify that the way to accomplish this is to place selfish desires and unworthy ambitions on the altar of sacrifice and service."[11]

Yes, it can be frightening. Sacrifice is – at best – uncomfortable. And – at worst – frightening. But we need not fear because God has made it clear:

"Have not I commanded thee? Be strong and of a good courage; be not afraid, neither be thou dismayed: for the Lord thy God is with thee whithersoever thou goest" (Joshua 1:9).

It is our mission to lean on Him, but then stand by ourselves. It requires steel determination. A resolve which commits us to a prompting and a soft, humble heart which seeks for His guidance in acting on that prompting. To act is to live our truth – a truth learned through Him.

CHAPTER 4

A Broken Heart

"Children may outgrow your lap, but never your heart."
Agiovanelli

Servie adjusted the glasses perched on her nose. She would check the numbers again. It had been about two years and she had put everything she could into her savings account. Working hard and getting by with the bare necessities. Always thinking of her children before purchasing anything. Living frugal was living for them. Her fingers punched the numbers on the calculator. Carefully she added the deposits.

She nodded her head – pleased with the results. She had already sent money to Zimbabwe for the food and schooling of the younger children. There was still a good amount leftover. Certainly, more than enough to purchase an airline ticket home.

There wasn't a single day that Servie didn't think about her children. Where were they? What were they wearing? She tried to picture it all in her mind. Her imagination helped her feel closer than the thousands of miles that separated them.

Servie had become comfortable in her new surroundings. Yes, it was very different. But the people were kind. She had found friendship. For the first time since leaving her village, she began to see a glimmer of new possibilities. Perhaps her children could join her. She promised herself she would find a way to make that happen. The details seemed overwhelming, but her mind and heart focused on the prospect. The freedoms and opportunities here in the states felt endless. She considered what that could mean for her children. A fighting chance. A bright future. No more living day-to-day in survival. Privilege and liberty would be theirs. Doors would be open. Open to hope.

It had been two years since she had seen Kimberly. Two long years since she had turned for one last look before boarding that plane. She could hardly ponder that moment. Just the thought brought fresh tears to her eyes. Her brother sent pictures of Kimberly and she heard the tiny voice over the phone. The pictures were nice, but her arms ached with the emptiness. How she longed to embrace that beautiful little girl.

Before Servie left Zimbabwe, she had discussed Kimberly's upbringing with her brother and sister-in-law. Because Kimberly was only 2-years-old, these two family members would assume the roles of dad and mom. They had other children and Servie wanted Kimberly to feel included. Servie never wanted Kimberly to feel as though she was different. Just loved as a member of this beautiful family. As a baby, she would not understand the relationships and her mother's absence. The other children were old enough to comprehend the situation. Servie knew in her heart that she would have her children all together again one day, but for now Kimberly would know her as "Auntie." It hurt to consider the idea, but she wanted the best for this little one.

Mlungisi's playful spirit served him well in his school. This youngest boy of hers was loved by students and teachers alike. His humor and love of anything sports made him a favorite. Servie's sister who worked at the boarding school and her family continued to support and cheer this child on and off the field. Oh, how she missed this silly little boy. He made her laugh. She couldn't wait to scoop him up into her arms.

Thembelihle was growing up to be a beautiful little girl. The schooling was going well, but she missed her mother. Servie's sister took pictures of Thembelihle. It made Servie weep and then smile to see them. Sorrow for the void of her absence. And sweet joy at the thought that Thembelihle was being loved and cared for by family. Everybody was trying to do their part. But Servie longed to hold this beautiful little girl. Oh, it had been too long.

The older children were doing well. Her oldest son Thabani was still living with Servie's uncle and studying hard at a college in South Africa. One day he would be a successful businessman. How proud she was of him. His younger brother, Thembelani, was also investing his time and energy studying in science. What a gift he would be to the world someday. His intelligence set him apart. She always loved the way this boy's mind worked. She had seen it blossoming at such a young age. Her oldest daughter Thandeka was still attending high school in the UK and living with Servie's sister. Servie spoke to these older children often and encouraged them to continue in their studies. She could see that they were making their way. Building their futures. How proud she was of them. The miles of distance tugged on her heart, but she dreamed that somehow, they would all come together.

. . .

Servie closed her eyes and leaned her head back against the seat. She must try to relax. This day had finally arrived. Her first flight back to Zimbabwe. Her emotions were scattered and raw.

The flight was opening up painful memories. Two years ago, she had taken the hardest walk of her life onto an airplane which would take her thousands of miles away from her children. The sound of the engine, the pilot making announcements, the flight attendants' heels walking up and down the aisle – it brought it all back. That pit in her stomach. The fear of leaving everything she knew. Once was enough. She didn't want to re-live those feelings. After all, this was a day for celebration. A long-awaited day to see the younger children again. Not on some computer screen, but truly see them. Feel them.

The pilot began his long descent into Zimbabwe. Servie leaned into the window. Familiar surroundings filled her soul. Oh, how she had missed this place. In just a few minutes, her feet would walk again in her village. She would be home.

Servie searched the faces in the crowd. Desperate to see them. Her heart pounded. Her eyes darting back and forth.

And then she saw her. Wide eyes and a shy smile. Servie put her hand over her mouth and sobbed as she lunged toward her beautiful little 4-year-old. Kimberly reached out and grabbed onto her. Together they clung to each other. Tears filled the eyes of family members. They all understood the significance of this moment. The sacrifice. The love.

Servie spent two weeks wrapped up in the lives of her three younger children and her family and friends. It was an incredible reunion in her little village. They laughed and they cried. Telling and re-telling stories of everything that had happened in the two years that Servie had been gone. Servie embraced her sweet angels. Taking advantage of every tender moment. Little Kimberly didn't want to let go.

"Auntie," she would cry as she held both arms toward her.

Servie smiled.

"I'm just running next door to see my friends!" she would explain.

But Kimberly didn't want to let go. There was a special bond there. Spirit to spirit this little one knew that something was different about *this* Auntie.

"Okay, come here with me," Servie said as she scooped her up into her arms. She placed Kimberly on her hip and walked out the door.

"We will go together."

. . .

Servie woke to the sound of the alarm clock. Back to work. The kids at the care facility were depending on her. Once again, she would care for those kids who could not care for themselves. Brian would wonder where she had been.

Leaving Zimbabwe had been terribly hard all over again. She hated walking away from those children. Looking back to see tears in their eyes at her last goodbye. A haunting moment. Servie cried the whole flight back. This would never get easier.

Servie returned with renewed determination to make this work. She poured her energy once again into working as many hours as her place of employment would offer. A friend had recommended an attorney who might be able to help her get Kimberly over to the United States. The paperwork was difficult and there were government rules and regulations that Servie didn't understand. Her other children were away at boarding schools or living in the UK. They were cared for and watched over by family. But her little baby. She must find a way to work and pay the schooling for the others with little Kimberly here. *There must be a way.*

"I'll do what I can to get the necessary paperwork completed," her attorney said. Servie wrote the check for his services and placed it on his desk.

Months flew by as Servie continued her routine. Work … scrimp … save. As her savings grew, so did hopes of bringing her children over. She continued to write checks to the attorney. He was having trouble getting the paperwork approved. This was not going to be easy. Surely God would know this deepest desire of Servie's heart and make this happen.

Perhaps she was to learn patience. The government in Zimbabwe was so difficult. Nothing was happening. Servie refused to allow despair to consume her thoughts. She was determined to continue pushing forward. Servie would continue to visit the children once a year and continue to support their needs. But she was growing weary. Hoping a window of opportunity would open soon. An opportunity to gather her children together in a free land. She would call the attorney again tomorrow.

. . .

Mlungisi smiled. Her youngest boy had just finished his last year of high school in Zimbabwe – an official 2007 graduate. He was 18 years old and ready to celebrate his success. He was so ready to go back to the village for a visit. He was looking forward to seeing his little sister Kimberly again. He packed his things up and thought about all the fun things he would do with his cousins and his friends. Just another few minutes and the passenger van would be here to take him home. What a great reunion this would be.

Some 7,000 miles away, Servie took a seat on the couch at work in Indiana. It was just after midnight and she was working a late shift at her job caring for older individuals. They were sleeping now and it was quiet in the assisted living home. Her mind ran down the list of duties she needed to conquer in the evening hours before they woke up.

It was a cold, crisp evening in November. Seven long years since she had turned and taken the longest walk of her life – a walk through the airport gate and onto the airplane which would carry her away from everything she knew and loved. Seven years of working and saving and sending money to her children who felt so very far away.

Suddenly her cellphone rang. It was her cousin.

"Servie," he said, "I just got a phone call from home."

Servie glanced at her watch. It was the middle of the night. This couldn't be good news. Her stomach dropped.

"They asked me to tell you that Mlungisi was in a car accident. The van ... it was going too fast. The driver lost control and overturned. I'm sorry Servie. He died at the scene."

Servie tried to stand and felt her knees buckle. She exploded with disbelief and horror. An unimaginable pain pierced her heart. She fell to the ground howling ... screaming.

The manager heard the outcry. She raced over and grabbed the phone. Learned of the situation and arranged for cousins to drive Servie back to her home.

Servie dipped into her savings account and purchased a flight to Zimbabwe. It was three long days before she could get there. Her mother was visiting in New York City and arranged to meet her at the airport to take the last leg of the trip with her. All funeral plans were being made by family there in Zimbabwe. Servie emptied her savings account to pay for the required arrangements.

Servie found a moment by herself the night before the funeral. She wrote a letter to Mlungisi. A final tribute which she would display next to his body at the services.

Mlungisi,

May 29, 1989 was a beautiful and blessed day for me because that was the day you were born. When I held you in my arms, my heart overflowed with love, joy and pride. I guess the Lord also loved you way too much – so much that he wanted you back in heaven after only 18 short years. We had plans, never to be carried out. With school over and your passport out, you and I should have been working out the details of your "coming to America," but it was never to be. Mlungisi, you are physically gone from me, but you will live on in my heart and soul, my beloved son forever, and we will surely meet again. I trust you in the hands of the Lord. Rest in God's arms peacefully.

Your loving mother
Servie

The village gathered together in mourning. How could this happen again to this family? First Servie's father. Death by car accident. Then Servie's husband was taken. Death by cruel coincidence. Now her son. It didn't seem fair. Sweet Mlungisi was still so young. His bright life still ahead of him.

Servie returned to the states grief-stricken. Her heart felt heavy and cold. Nothing seemed to matter anymore. Life was dreary and dark. She tried to continue in her mission to provide for the other children. To find her focus. But it was so hard. The flight and the funeral expenses had drained her savings. The cloud of despair and hopelessness moved in and blinded Servie of any future hope. She cried each night into her pillow and woke each morning fighting anguish. Fighting to make any sense of this. Fighting to take another step forward.

. . .

Grief. It is not always easy to give voice to thoughts and emotions inside. These swell up to tears and down to numbness and then repeat. At times, it seems like no one else understands or could fathom such deep pain.

It is helpful to know that grief is the natural by-product of love. We cannot selflessly love another person and not grieve at his suffering or eventual death. The only way to avoid the grief would be to not experience the love. And it is this love that gives life its richness and meaning.

> *Grief is the last act of love*
> *we can give to those we love.*
> *Where there is deep grief*
> *there was great love.*
> Unknown

Supplication and prayers plead for mercy. For relief. Emotions swirl within our hearts and mind and we beg for Him to help us understand. What a grieving parent can expect to receive from the Lord in response to earnest prayer may not necessarily be an elimination of grief so much as a sweet reassurance that, whatever his or her circumstances, one's child is in the tender care of a loving Heavenly Father.

We should never doubt the goodness of God, even if we do not know why. *Why* did our child die when we prayed so hard that she would live? *Why* are we struggling with this tragedy when others relate miraculous healing experiences for their loved ones? Natural and understandable questions. But these are also questions that go begging in mortality. The Lord has said simply, *"My ways (are) higher than your ways, and my thoughts than your thoughts"* (Isaiah 55:9).

Still as mortals here on earth, we quite naturally want to know the why. In pressing on and on for answers, we may forget that mortality was designed, in a manner of speaking, as the season of unanswered questions. Mortality has a different, more narrowly defined purpose. It is a proving ground. A probationary state. A time to walk by faith. And a time to prepare to meet God.

When we soften our hearts and nurture humility and submissiveness, we may comprehend a fullness of the intended mortal experience and put ourselves in a frame of mind and heart to receive the promptings of the Spirit. We put ourselves in a position to let the "why" questions go unanswered for now, or perhaps even to ask, "Why not?"[1]

It is ultimately trusting not our own wisdom, but the Lord's. We have tunnel vision. The Lord sees the past, the present and the future. With broken hearts, we must turn our questions over to Him, and position ourselves to heal. One day at a time.

. . .

Thabani dragged himself to work. He had not been himself

lately. Always tired. He thought of his mother. He thought of his younger siblings. And he thought of his little brother Mlungisi, whose death two years ago had been such a hardship on all of them. He shook his head as if to resolve himself and focus. It was 2009 and he had a job to do. He must continue as the oldest son to work to help his mother support the family. When his father died, he felt a responsibility as the oldest boy to contribute money toward the younger children's needs. He had found a good job in South Africa and had made the decision to put college off for himself. It was a dream to continue his education and make his mother proud, but that would have to wait. She needed his help.

Thabani had been to the doctors in South Africa and learned that his kidneys were suffering. The medicine had helped for some time, but he was getting weaker and weaker. Where was his strength? He wondered if he was slowly losing the battle.

Servie called to talk to him often. She was worried about Thabani. Every few days she would call him to encourage and uplift. Trying to reassure him.

"It will all be okay Thabani. I'll help you pay for the medicine and the hospital."

She also needed to hear her own words of comfort, as if saying them out loud somehow made it all possible. Maybe if she heard her own voice say it, God would hear it, too. Servie had asked her mother to pray for Thabani. She couldn't lose another son. Her heart couldn't take it.

Thabani's health worsened over the next few months. Eventually he was unable to work. Servie's uncle would often call in the night when Servie was working the late shift. He would call to give updates on Thabani's condition, sometimes to say the hospital needed more money.

Thabani was frustrated. He didn't want to be a burden. He wanted to help his mother, not be a cause for worry. For awhile the medicine seemed to be working, but recently his energy had spiraled down to almost nothing. Breathing was an effort.

Back in Indiana, Servie stood by the window watching the horizon. The sun was just coming up. It cast a warm glow on the trees and the garden. The sky showing small signs of light. Everything was so quiet and still. Such serenity. Quite different from last night's restless sleep. Her anxious mind had allowed only minutes of sleep.

The ring of Servie's phone jolted her reflection.

"Mom ... mom ..."

It was a quiet, weak voice. Thabani's voice. He was trying to tell her something. But there was nothing left. It was all he could whisper. Two final words.

. . .

Servie threw herself onto the bed, dropped her face into the pillow and howled. She felt herself crumbling. The depression rolled in like a dark cloud and wrapped its cold arms around Servie's heart. Days felt like weeks. Her moods were unpredictable and erratic. One minute numb. The next screaming and crying with grief. Life was barely worth living.

This tragic, heartbreaking story had become hers. Each chapter in her story adding to the mound of heartache left before. Would it ever end? Was there any faith? Any promise of something better? Servie's song was silent. There was no melody at all.

The family pulled together to rescue. Servie's sister came from New York City to care for her. The heartache and worry had consumed Servie's life. Everywhere she looked there were reminders … darkness. Waves of anxiety came crashing into daily events. The phone became the enemy. Phone numbers from Zimbabwe meant bad news. Just the ringing of the phone set her off. Servie couldn't stop shaking. And her nerves were raw and tight.

"Anxiety and depression," the doctors said.

Servie spent some time in the hospital getting stabilized on medication. Once home she tried to control her environment. Often, she simply turned the phone off. Just talking to anyone in Zimbabwe brought up emotions. Family members knew to leave messages. Daily tears were the norm. Not a day went by that she didn't think of those two boys.

Servie's mother pulled together a prayer circle. They would call Servie at a set time to pray together on the phone. Sisters, cousins, daughters. Everyone took a turn praying to God for understanding. For peace. Everyone except Servie. She couldn't pray. Not now. The words weren't there. Over and over she held the phone to her ear as the others prayed. Finding some comfort in their faith. But for now, she could only listen. And hope.

. . .

Grief, I've learned,
is really just love.
It's all the love you want to give but cannot.
All of that unspent love gathers up in the
Corners of your eyes, the lump in your throat,
And in that hollow part of your chest.

Grief is just love
With no place to go.

Unknown

In James 5:16 we read, "*Confess your faults one to another, and pray one for another, that ye may be healed. The effectual fervent prayer of a righteous man availeth much.*" What an incredible blessing to learn that we can communicate directly with our Heavenly Father. He is always ready to listen. To bless. Though we may not yet be able to express words, our prayers can be heard from the heart. It is the first step toward a deeper relationship and trust in God.

Prayer is the soul's sincere desire,
Uttered or unexpressed,
The motion of a hidden fire
That trembles in the breast.

Prayer is the burden of a sigh,
The falling of a tear,
The upward glancing of an eye
When none but God is near[2]

We pray to find shelter from the storm that screams around us. There is a safe harbor where we can find peace. Heavenly Father, who knows when even a sparrow falls[3], knows of *our* heartache and suffering. He loves us and wants the best for us. And while He does not always intervene in the course of events, He has promised peace to the faithful – even in their trials and tribulations.

That peace may not be tangible, but felt within the soul. Jesus comforts us when He said, *"Peace I leave with you, my peace I give unto you: not as the world giveth, give I unto you. Let not your heart be troubled, neither let it be afraid"* (John 14:27).

Despite the pain and sorrow within us, we must reach upward and draw close to the Lord Jesus Christ. He is the Son of God – an eternal king. Above all others, He is one who knows suffering and so certainly bears a special love for those who hurt. We read of so many examples in the scriptures. Every word to the meek and discouraged was one of compassion and encouragement. He brought a healing balm to the sick. Those who yearned for hope and a caring touch received it from the hand of this King of Kings – this Creator of ocean, earth and sky.

Today Jesus Christ stands at the right hand of our Heavenly Father. Do you suppose that today He is any less inclined to aid those who suffer, who are sick, or who pray from deep within their soul? Certainly not. His love and compassion live as He does. Though He does not currently minister on the earth, He is but a prayer away.

Consider the butterfly. Wrapped tightly in its cocoon, the developing chrysalis must struggle with all its might to break its confining prison. The butterfly might think, "Why must I suffer so? Why can't I simply, in the twinkling of an eye, just become a butterfly?"

These thoughts are contrary to the Creator's design. The struggle to break out of the cocoon strengthens and develops the butterfly so it can fly. The butterfly needs that adversity to gain the strength to achieve its destiny. Now it can become something extraordinary.

Adversity also can strengthen and refine us. We develop character. Even when called to sail through troubled waters, this adversity will shape our divine potential. Figuratively, we are given wings to fly.

We are stronger than we think. Our eternal spirits have immeasurable capacity. God does not wish us to cower or wallow in our misery. Certainly, there is a time for that. But he expects us to square our shoulders, roll up our sleeves and overcome heartbreak. That kind of spirit – that blend of faith and hard work – is the spirit we should emulate as we seek our Heavenly Father in prayer. Seek to reach a safe harbor in our own lives. And seek to find our wings.[4]

. . .

Thembelani was flourishing in the UK. He had studied medicine and physics and had received honors and acknowledgement in the school papers. His success in education led to a lucrative job and he was making good money. The death of two brothers had been terribly difficult, but Thembelani was 34 years old and in the prime of his life. He would forge ahead in their memory. He was always willing to help support family when necessary. Life was good.

Suddenly other opportunities opened up. He had heard about the gold mines in Zimbabwe. There was a lot of money to be made. Stories were circulating about others who had opened up a mining business and struck gold – and wealth. Thembelani was always bright. He had the brainpower to do whatever he wanted and the drive to go after a challenge. The idea of opening up his own gold mining business peaked his interest. And he had the money to make a good start.

Thembelani knew Zimbabwe. He had that advantage. After a good amount of research, he decided to leave for Zimbabwe with the money he'd earned and start a new business. Gold mining.

Servie was nervous about this new career interest. She worried about his safety in returning to Zimbabwe. He had been successful in graduate school and Servie reminded him of that when he mentioned the mining opportunity. There was a sinking feeling she couldn't quite shake.

In Indiana, it was a cold day in the winter of 2011 and Servie hurried up the walkway. Despite what she had been through, Servie would continue to love others. Serving others kept her mind off her own losses and worries. She had recently heard that a friend in Indiana had lost her mother. Servie knocked on the door. She was there to love and to comfort. She understood grief and was certain she could share some insight. Help her friend through the process.

A few minutes after visiting with her friend, Servie's phone rang.

"Servie, are you by yourself?"

It was her sister.

"No," Servie answered. "I'm here at my friend's house. Why?"

"It's Thembelani ... I'm so sorry. It's terrible Servie. They got him ... somebody bad got him. They killed him, Servie! For his money and his gold."

Servie fell back into a chair. She pulled her knees up and hugged them tight as sobs racked her body. Servie shook her head in disbelief and rocked herself as if somehow that would give comfort.

"Not again. My boys – all my beautiful boys," she wailed.

It had been a whirlwind. Servie almost couldn't make sense

of anything. She had called her boss at work to explain that she needed to leave immediately for Zimbabwe … again. Another death. Another son. It sounded implausible as she spoke the words. But the absences had far exceeded the policy limits.

"Take some time and pull yourself together," her boss said. "Call me in six months and I'll see about giving your job back. We are really sorry."

Friends in the community had heard the unthinkable news. They rallied and pulled together funds to cover Servie's airfare. What little she had left in savings might cover the funeral expenses. She was grateful for their kind generosity.

. . .

Servie walked into the police station in Zimbabwe.

"I am the mother of Thembelani," she whispered.

They quietly escorted her to a room and told her to have a seat.

The door opened and an officer walked in and sat down in the chair across the table from Servie. He looked directly at her and quietly spoke.

"We have the two men," he said. "Tell us what to do with them."

The laws were obscure and justice was ambiguous. They were looking to her for direction. She raised her eyes and met the officer's gaze. Spoke what was in her heart.

"Let them go," she said. "Putting them in jail will not bring my son back."

The officer nodded his head. "You're sure?"

"Yes," she answered, "but I want to talk to them."

Minutes later the door swung open and a man was shoved into the chair across from Servie. He was the ringleader.

Silence filled the room. Nobody dared to make a sound. The air was thick with a stale odor of sweat and fear. Servie had rehearsed this in her mind. She willed her voice to speak.

"Why?" she said. She could feel a wave of emotion rising up in her throat. "Why …?"

The man kept his head down. He couldn't look at her. A true coward. Finally, he muttered a response.

"I'm sorry," he simply said.

Servie felt a cold tear escape from the corner of her eye. It traveled down her hot cheek then found a path over her chin and down her neck. She didn't bother to wipe it away. Just let it fall. A cold, wet symbol of the sorrow and the turmoil building in her chest.

Servie stood up. Her legs were shaking so hard they nearly collapsed. She steadied herself then slowly grabbed her purse and walked out. Never looking back.

She would leave behind the anger. Leave it sitting there in that cold, hard chair across from that murderer. The anger would not bring her son back. But it would destroy her. She knew it would. She could already feel its hot, angry fingers trying to strangle her heart.

God knew she would grieve. Oh, how she would grieve. But this day Servie made a choice that felt right for her. Servie chose to walk. Servie chose to save her soul.

. . .

We read in the Old Testament of Daniel and his young friends who were suddenly thrust from their own security into a foreign and intimidating world. When Shadrach, Meshach and Abednego refused to bow down and worship a golden image set up by the king, a furious King Nebuchadnezzar told them they would immediately be cast into a burning fiery furnace. *"And who is that God that shall deliver you out of my hands?"* (Daniel 3:15)

These three young men quickly and confidently responded, *"If it be so, our God whom we serve is able to deliver us from the burning fiery furnace, and **he will deliver us out of thine hand, O king."** *They then continued demonstrating that they fully understood what faith is, *"**But if not**, be it known unto thee, O king, that we will not serve thy gods, nor worship the golden image which thou hast set up"* (Daniel 3:17-18). What an example of true faith.

These young men knew that they could trust God – even if things didn't turn out the way they hoped. Faith is more than an acknowledgement that God lives. Faith is total trust in Him. Faith is believing that we do not understand all things, but He does. Faith is knowing that our power is limited, but His is not.

We each have the agency to choose. And in this life He tests us by allowing us to be challenged. We are assured that He *"will not suffer you to be tempted above that ye are able ..."* (1 Corinthians 10:13). None of us would ever seek tribulation, but the Lord will strengthen us. The *"but if nots"* can ultimately become our greatest blessings.

The Apostle Paul also learned this significant lesson after decades of dedicated missionary work. He said, *"... we glory in tribulations also: knowing that tribulation worketh patience; And patience, experience; and experience, hope: And hope maketh not ashamed; because the love of God is shed abroad in our hearts by the Holy Ghost which is given unto us"* (Romans 5:3-5). Paul knew that when he met his challenges the Lord's way, his faith increased. He testifies, "*Most gladly therefore will I rather glory in my infirmities, that the power of Christ may rest upon me. Therefore I take pleasure in infirmities, in reproaches, in necessities, in persecutions, in distresses for Christ's sake: for when I am weak, then am I strong*" (2 Corinthians 12:9-10).

Our scriptures and our history are filled with accounts of God's great men and women who accomplished marvelous things by trusting in the Lord and keeping His commandments. They exercised faith even when they didn't know how the Lord was shaping them. In the midst of all those glorious outcomes hoped for and expected, there were always the "*but if nots.*" Some were mocked and scourged. Others were stoned and tormented. These great men and women believed that He would deliver them, *but if not*, they demonstrated that they would trust and be true.

It is our test. We are expected to do all that we can do. He not only does the rest – His grace makes up all the difference.

"Our God will deliver us from ridicule and persecution, *but if not* … . Our God will deliver us from sickness and disease, *but if not* … . He will deliver us from loneliness, depression, or fear, *but if not* … . Our God will deliver us from threats, accusations, and insecurity, *but if not* … . He will deliver us from death or impairment of loved ones, *but if not, … we will trust in the Lord.*[5]

A strong message so easily spoken. More difficult to live. But we must rise above. A song of heartbreak. A song so tender and weak it's barely heard. Yet … still a song.

CHAPTER 5

Adjust Your Sails

"A smooth sea never made a great sailor."
Franklin D. Roosevelt

Servie thrust her hands into the cool dirt. She poked her fingers deep into the soil and carved out a small hole. Gently, she placed the seedling and pushed the soil back into place. She patted the ground as a final gesture of confidence. "*That should do,*" she thought. Some extra care and attention over the next few weeks and her garden should respond with fresh vegetables.

It had been months since Servie had cultivated her garden in Indiana. She had left in a frenzied blur last month, took the first flight to Zimbabwe, which would deliver her to handle yet another unthinkable tragedy. A horrendous, violent detour from the mission she was living. Now she was back in the states. Time to find more work. The funeral expenses and the loss of her job had completely drained her savings. She had almost nothing.

It felt good to work in the garden. It was a place of peace. Faith that if her hands could grow this tiny seedling into food, then maybe her heart could grow again. Feel again. Something deep inside promised her there was hope. Perhaps a glimmer of happiness in her future was possible. She yearned to find it.

Servie sat back and brushed the dirt off her hands. She pulled her knees up tight to her chest. It reminded her of home. She forced her mind to draw on good, positive memories from previous trips to Zimbabwe.

The two older girls, Thandeka and Thembelihle were doing well in graduate school in the UK. She was so proud of them. They, too, were hurting from the loss of their brothers. But they seemed to be handling their emotions. Perhaps the routine of their schooling and blossoming careers was a healthy distraction. Servie loved these girls. What beautiful young women they had become. The sacrifice to pay for their education and care was worth every bead of sweat. "*I would do it all over again,*" thought Servie … *for them.*

Kimberly had flourished in her elementary years. She loved her family in Zimbabwe. The cousins that played and cared for her growing up were brothers and sisters in her mind. She belonged to this little family and felt loved. She, too, was saddened by the passing of her "Auntie's" sons. One day she would know of the true blood relationships in her life. But not yet. Servie didn't want to disrupt her world of belonging.

At 13, Kimberly was finally old enough to attend one of the better boarding schools which began instruction in the 8th grade. It was a 4-hour drive away from the village. Servie's sister worked at the boarding school and promised to look after Kimberly during the week. Kimberly would then be able to return home to the village on holidays or weekends if homesickness was an issue. The boarding school would offer a significantly better education for Kimberly and if she performed well it offered scholarship opportunities for colleges outside of Zimbabwe. Servie knew that it opened up future doors for this little one. So, just like the others, she would find a way to pay the tuition.

Servie's thoughts took her back to the last visit to Zimbabwe months ago. Servie had spent a quiet moment talking with Kimberly about her new schooling. Kimberly reached into a bag and pulled out some knit booties.

"Look, Auntie," she smiled. "These were a present from my mom. She wants me to have warm feet when I sleep at school. She brought these to me with a blanket. And when they have visiting days at the school, Mom always brings me cookies."

Servie choked back the tears. Tears of gratitude for a sister-in-law who loved this child as her own. And tears of heartache that she wasn't the parent who tucked this daughter in at night.

Servie held the booties in her hands. Promised herself that she would visualize them each night keeping her little one warm and cozy. She hugged Kimberly and handed her the booties.

"That's wonderful my dear."

A blast of cool breeze on the back of her neck brought Servie back to the present. The Indiana sun had dropped below the horizon and the air suddenly had a cool bite to it. Time to get back inside. Darkness was rolling in. She would tend again to this garden tomorrow.

Servie climbed into bed and turned out the light. Nights were the hardest. She dreaded the quiet evenings when thoughts pushed their way to the front. Negative, dark thoughts. There was not a single night that she didn't think of her three boys. It was a nightly tug-of-war. A contest of happy memories and moments fighting with the intimate realities of death.

Her little Mlungisi – oh, how he used to make her smile. Such a curious, funny one.

"Mom, did you ever go to school?" he would ask.

"Why?" answered Servie.

"Because Mom – all my auntie's are teachers. How come you're not a teacher? You always want me to go to school and do my homework," he cried.

Servie cupped his little face in her hands.

"I don't want you to be like me, Mlungisi," Servie disclosed. "I want you to be better."

Servie considered her future. If this nightmare would ever end, just maybe things could change. She smiled as she thought of his questioning face. *One day maybe I'll go to college … just for him.*

Suddenly she felt the familiar wave of doom creep into her space. Darkness consumed her. Flashbacks of sickness. Doctors and hospitals and bottles of pills. Thabani's quiet, weak voice. "Mom …"

Visions of violence and murder. The madness and the unfairness of it all. Had Thembelani run from them? Did he suffer? She would never know all the details and her imagination tried to fill them in the blanks. She had forgiven the murderers. There was peace with that, but the pain of emptiness fought for control. The boulder-sized knot in her stomach twisted. It felt dark and heavy.

Servie squeezed her eyes tight and pulled her pillow up around her face, as if to shut out the bitterness. She took a deep breath and blew it out hard. Willed herself to allow a glimmer of faith chase away the fear. This mania would not win. *Tomorrow is a new day.* She pushed that thought to the forefront and held on tight. The sun would come out again. And there would be light. With every ounce of strength and courage she would rise and look for a new job.

"*Tomorrow is a new day*" … a final, desperate thought before Servie drifted off to sleep.

. . .

You're shattered
Like you've never been before
The life you knew
In a thousand pieces on the floor
And words fall short in times like these
When this world drives you to your knees
You think you're never gonna get back
To the you that used to be

Tell your heart to beat again
Close your eyes and breathe it in
Let the shadows fall away
Step into the light of grace
Yesterday's a closing door
You don't live there anymore
Say goodbye to where you've been
And tell your heart to beat again

Beginning
Just let that word wash over you
It's alright now
Love's healing hands have pulled you through
So get back up, take step one
Leave the darkness, feel the sun
Cause your story's far from over
And your journey's just begun[1]

What is faith? The Bible dictionary states that "*faith is to hope for things which are not seen, but which are true ...* and that the Lord himself possessed *"in their fullness all the attributes of love, knowledge, justice, mercy, unchangeableness, power, and every other needful thing, so as to enable the mind of man to place confidence in him without reservation."* It is more than belief because it stirs us to action. A focus which allows us to move forward despite past or current events.

Faith is seeing light with your heart when all your eyes see is darkness.[2] A perfect reminder that we find on framed quotes and refrigerator magnets. A description of seeing in an extraordinary way.

So often children are our teachers. They have an inner desire to do right, a natural sense of worth, the ability to be happy, a capacity to love, and an innate sense of wisdom, but their foundational and crowning attribute is a natural, deep, and trusting faith. How many of us have been panicked with a problem and had a young child remind us to pray about it? How many of us have heard a child pray for a friend or neighbor who is sick or sad? When children have been taught about God, their buckets spontaneously fill up with faith.

How much faith do we adults have in our buckets? Are we full, empty, or somewhere in between? Many of us may recognize that it has been a while since we have been as close to God as we should be. Perhaps we feel there have been too many hurts, mistakes and regrets along the way. It would do us well to rediscover faith like that of our children.

The scriptures assure us that *"... the just shall live by his faith"* (Habakkuk 2:4). For every person who says we cannot change, there are others whose lives are evidence of the transforming power of Christ. For every person who finds fault with organized religion, there are others who show with words and actions that it is possible to find and live at a higher level. And for every person who claims that faith is a weakness, there are others who testify that faith is the source of true inner strength.[3]

We develop greater faith as we pass through trials. The trials and adversity can be preparatory to becoming born anew. And that faith becomes priceless. *"That the trial of your faith, being much more precious than of gold that perisheth, though it be tried with fire, might be found unto praise and honour and glory at the appearing of Jesus Christ"* (1 Peter 1:7).

The refining process itself often seems cruel and hard. There seems to be some measure of anguish, sorrow and often heartbreak for everyone, including those who earnestly seek to do right and be faithful. But this refining process of change allows our soul to become like soft clay in the hands of the Master in building lives of faith, usefulness, beauty and strength. For some, the refiner's fire causes a loss of belief and faith in God, but those with an eternal perspective understand that such refining is part of the perfection process. One in which we become more like Him.[4]

The refining process can seem exceptionally difficult when we live the gospel principle of forgiveness. Forgiveness is a cleansing of the soul when harsh realities and feelings have consumed us. The scriptures are clear: *"Let all bitterness, and wrath, and anger, and clamour, and evil speaking, be put away from you, with all malice: And be ye kind one to another, tenderhearted, forgiving one another, even as God for Christ's sake hath forgiven you"* (Ephesians 4:31-32).

Forgiveness is a glorious, healing principle. At one time or another we will all be the victim to someone else's careless actions, hurtful conduct, or even sinful behavior. But God has prepared a way to help us navigate these sometimes-turbulent experiences of life. We can forgive! Yes, we may be a victim once, but we need not be a victim twice by carrying the burden of hate, bitterness, pain, resentment, or even revenge. If we forgive, we can be free!

The unforgiving heart harbors so much needless pain. When we apply the Savior's Atonement, He will soften our heart and help us to change. Many want to forgive, but we find it very hard to do. We may think *that person did wrong … they deserve punishment … where is the justice …?* It is a mistake to think that if we forgive, somehow justice will not be served and punishments will be avoided. God will mete out a punishment that is fair. Applying the Savior's Atonement is handing it over to Him.

As victims, if we are faithful, we can take great comfort and find peace in knowing that God will compensate us for every injustice we experience. Elder Joseph B. Wirthlin stated: "*The Lord compensates the faithful for every loss. … Every tear today will eventually be returned a hundredfold with tears of rejoicing and gratitude.*"[5] Remember that we are all growing spiritually, but we are all at different levels. Certainly, those who are less spiritually mature may indeed make serious mistakes – yet none of us should be defined only by the worst thing we have done. God is the perfect judge because He sees beneath the surface and knows all.[6]

This cleansing of our soul and the act of turning it over to Him is a promised pathway to peace. Faith allows us to move forward. And faith is key to a softer, gentler heart. A heart which is just like His.

. . .

Servie continued to reach out to everyone she knew. Friends

from the care facility where she had previously worked. Friends she had met in the community. Friends at the local church. She was willing to take any kind of work – part time or full time. And she was determined to spread the word as quickly as possible. Certainly, something would come up if she did her part. She was depending on that. And so, she knocked on doors and made phone calls daily.

Family members rallied together to provide support. They were worried about Servie. Her voice sounded strained over the phone. Emails and texts were short and to the point. She just didn't have the energy to engage in small talk. Her spark was gone.

Three sons gone. No job. It had been too much.

"Where are you God?" Servie thought. Perhaps prayers were useless. They felt futile and worthless. She had prayed after losing her youngest boy in a car accident. Surely God heard her. Heard her cries and screams and felt her despair. Yet, she had lost another … and then another. *I am in the middle of the river. I am lost.* She felt beaten. Abandoned. Forgotten.

Servie glanced at the clock. Just a few minutes and she would receive a conference call. It had to be scheduled because she wouldn't accept unannounced phone calls from Zimbabwe anymore. Too many traumatic calls had come from Zimbabwe. The anxiety just from seeing the country code on the phone was too much.

The shrill ring caught Servie's attention. She sat down and picked up the phone.

"Servie, it's Mom. Honey – your sisters are on the line. You don't need to pray until you're ready. You just listen. Our prayer is your prayer."

Mom in Zimbabwe, a sister in New York City, and two sisters

in the UK. It was a family circle of love. They pulled together in faith. They pulled together in prayer. And they pulled together for Servie. Each of them taking a turn – leading the group in a heartfelt, honest talk with God. Praising and thanking Him for the blessings in their lives. And asking Him for courage and strength to move forward in this difficult time. Sometimes it lifted Servie's spirits. She looked forward to this. Loved these beautiful women and their desire to help. And maybe one day she would be ready to take a turn and pray. But not today. She leaned back, closed her eyes, and listened.

. . .

Sometimes the battle is long and arduous. The duration can be years – even a lifetime. Or it hits hard and fast – nearly taking our breath away. A fight through a difficulty which takes us by surprise and has the effect of breaking up those perfectly placed puzzle pieces.

We learn and study His gospel. We begin to understand that life here on earth is a test. Sometimes we are able to look backward and see the good in past trials. We recognize how we have grown, how paths were redirected, see how puzzle pieces were placed by His hand and not by ours. It bolsters our faith to reflect and perceive the blessings that have bloomed amid the mud. Our faith is strengthened and noted.

Ultimately, though, we learn the real test is not having faith in the beginning or the end of the battle. The real test is having faith in the middle. Unable to see any possibility of the end. Unable to find our way. Having and clinging to faith when we are *in the middle of the river.* That is the true test of faith.

Over and over again we read in the scriptures of faith conquering fear in extreme circumstances of hopelessness. Surely the children of Israel felt enormous fear as their eyes beheld the Egyptians marching after them. They cried out to the Lord because they felt all was lost. With the sea in front of them and chariots behind them, it seemed all was lost. But Moses counseled them:

"Fear ye not, stand still, and see the salvation of the Lord, which he will shew to you to day: for the Egyptians whom ye have seen to day, ye shall see them again no more for ever. The Lord shall fight for you, and ye shall hold your peace. And the Lord said unto Moses, Wherefore criest thou unto me? speak unto the children of Israel, that they go forward" (Exodus 14:13-15).

What a pattern to follow when we are fighting in the middle. Taking our fear and intentionally replacing it with faith. Standing still enough to trust that He will whisper and guide our steps. Trusting that the Lord will save us and forge the path back to Him. Believing that He will fight right beside us. And finding the strength and faith to take a step forward. A pathway from darkness to light. Even when we cannot see the way. A pattern and a way to find hope when all forces are against us.

To stay in the fight – trusting that the Lord will deliver – is a form of sacrifice. Often, we are tempted to flee the situation. Take the quickest exit. It is a sacrifice to live the principle of faith. New and unexpected storylines take us in a different direction. As we live it, we feel it. And ultimately, we are changed by it if we stay the course.

Our reaction to this unexpected direction is key. Dieter F. Uchtdorf said, *"It is your reaction to adversity, not the adversity itself, that determines how your life's story will develop."*[7] When we are at a crossroads in life, sometimes the only decision we can make is one of attitude. An attitude of happiness.

Once again children show us the example. They are naturally happy and they don't wait for it – they create happiness. Psalm 128:1-2 promises that *"every one that feareth the Lord; that walketh in His ways … happy shalt thou be."* This promised happiness comes from our relationship with and obedience to the Lord. As foolish adults, we think happiness comes from winning a competition, enjoying popularity, being blessed with good health, or having not experienced divorce or some form of abuse. This perceived happiness may seem forever out of our reach – *I'll be happy when I lose 10 pounds,* or *I'll be happy when I find a spouse,* or *I'll be happy when I get a raise.* Children create their happiness because they choose to be happy now.

There is a wise saying: *Happiness is a city in the state of mind.* Regardless of the state or nation in which they were born, children know the City of Happiness – it is their birthright. This perspective can make a huge difference to us.[8]

We all encounter storms in our lives. Life during the storm takes determination, some skill and a hefty dose of attitude. We may need to adjust our sails to get through. Make a few corrections. Change a few things.

We never hear an old sea captain boast that in all his experience he has never seen a squally sea or a heavy, storm-laden sky. Often stories are told of hearing the tempest shriek through the rigging and threaten to tear away the masts. His pride is in his skill and his experience, not in his luck. The sea never remains serene and calm with no ruffling waves for years at a time. Instead, inevitable storms are weathered with safety, love and trust. The old sea captain gains a new dose of wisdom and becomes better and better at adjusting those sails to endure the disturbance. We, too, like the sea captain will be forced to venture into the storms of life as we gain experience and wisdom.[9]

We have all heard the saying – Trouble is inevitable, but misery is optional. Thomas S. Monson explained, "*So much in life depends on our attitude. The way we choose to see things and respond to others makes all the difference. To do the best we can and then to choose to be happy about our circumstances, whatever they may be, can bring peace and contentment. We can't direct the wind, but we can adjust the sails. For maximum happiness, peace, and contentment, may we choose a positive attitude.*"[10]

Storms are not simple. But if we were to simplify our reaction, it would be to trust. Trust that we don't have the big picture. We don't have the broad view. Only He does. So we have to take our tunnel vision and turn it over to the One who has a panorama.

Cause what if Your blessings come through raindrops
What if Your healing comes through tears?
And what if a thousand sleepless nights
Are what it takes to know You're near?

What if my greatest disappointments
Or the aching of this life
Is the revealing of a greater thirst
This world can't satisfy?

And what if trials of this life
The rain, the storms, the hardest nights
Are Your mercies in disguise?[11]

. . .

Over time, a combination of persistent efforts and a community of friends who loved Servie enabled her to find some part-time work. A good friend referred her to Rod, a good church-going man who had two small children. He had work opportunities abroad and would need some extra help for a couple of years. This was perfect for Servie. She craved pouring her love and energy into children. She would care for them each week and more often when Rod traveled for work. It was a blessing. An opportunity which helped both Rod and Servie.

Eventually, the travel slowed down and Rod needed less and less help. The hours became more scarce. Servie needed more hours.

"I understand that you don't require as much help now," Servie said.

Rod met her gaze. He felt badly about that. But she was right. His traveling was complete and that allowed him much more flexibility with the children. He knew she needed more income.

"If you know somebody who is looking for help – could you let me know?" asked Servie.

Rod rubbed his forehead as he considered the request. His mind thought through the list of friends, work colleagues, people in his church. Surely there was someone. Suddenly the thought came. He turned and looked at Servie with wide eyes.

"There is someone! I have a friend, Angela, and she just came back from some time in Arizona and she is looking for help. She's here to stay in Indiana for awhile. Oh, Servie! This might work. I'll reach out to her and give you her contact information."

A few days later Servie knocked on Angela's door. This was a beautiful home. Servie took a deep breath and steadied herself. She hoped this might be good.

The door opened. There stood a lovely, elegant woman with light hair and clear, blue eyes. She smiled.

"Hello. You must be Servie. I'm Angela. Come on in."

Angela led Servie over to a chair and motioned for her to sit. Servie immediately felt at ease with this woman. There was kindness in her eyes and compassion in her voice. Something felt right.

Angela looked at this woman and considered her options. Angela didn't have the best first impression – Servie was late. Her inclination was to thank her for her time and find someone else. She had strict expectations for work ethic and standards. "*Perhaps a cultural difference between Zimbabwe time and American time,*" Angela thought. All logic told her to kindly dismiss her. But a small voice told her to be patient with this woman.

Angela talked about the help she would need. Cleaning. Organizing. Managing various affairs of the house. Angela's husband traveled quite often for work. Between caring for her child and her own work and travels, she needed help handling it all.

Now it was Servie's turn. She talked about her experience at the care facility. Loving and caring for those children in assisted homes. Making a difference in their lives. She talked about working for Rod. Helping him manage his household while he traveled. She briefly mentioned her desire to work so that she could send money back home to care for her children.

Angela saw the emotion. She saw dark eyes that had seen too much. Servie had a beautiful smile that lit up a room, but Angela sensed something deeper. "*There is a story behind this woman's face,*" she thought. A story that she hoped to learn. "*In time,*" Angela thought. A small stirring in her heart told her to trust and help Servie.

Angela smiled and leaned forward.

"How soon can you start?"

. . .

We were sent here to succeed. The plan was set up for it. It was never God's intent for us to survive life's battles on our own. We have His spirit to guide us in making decisions and navigating unmarked paths. We have his word in scripture that gives direction and purpose, and we have earthly angels who cross our paths and make a profound difference in our lives. Sometimes we recognize it when it happens. Other times we look back and see the miracle.

We each have that divine nature within us. James E. Faust believes that God sent women to earth with some qualities in extra capacity. He observed that femininity "*is the divine adornment of humanity. It finds expression in your ... capacity to love, your spirituality, delicacy, radiance, sensitivity, creativity, charm, graciousness, gentleness, dignity, and quiet strength. It is manifest differently in each woman, but each ... possesses it.*"[12]

We recognize women who understand and are grateful to be a daughter of God by their attitude. They know that the errand of angels is given to women. They desire to be on God's errand to love His children and minister to them.[13]

The scriptures are full of descriptive words and phrases which describe the Savior's arms – arms of mercy, encircling, open, outstretched, extended. He is always there to embrace us with his love and mercy. Sometimes He uses the arms of others to love and to guide. People placed on our path to lift us up. Helpers on our right, on our left and all around us. When these selfless people serve *us*, they serve *Him*. He feels the comfort given as if it had been given to Him.[14]

What is our story? The story of our search for happiness is written in such a way that if we continue to trust God and follow His commandments through the challenging times, even those times of hardship and despair will bring us closer to the ultimate happiness we are seeking.[15] The Savior said, "*In the world ye shall have tribulation: but be of good cheer; I have overcome the world*" (John 16:33). The better we understand the purpose of our existence, the better we are in a position to feel joy. It is holding fast to our faith. It is forgiving others of hurt and pain imposed on our life. It is adjusting the sails as we watch for the Lord to direct the wind.

. . .

Servie embraced her work at Angela's. She was eager to learn and do the very best she could to help. As time passed, her work became a joy instead of a necessity. She found herself looking forward to it each morning. Angela was friendly and gracious. She was genuinely interested in Servie's life. And Servie found herself opening up more and more to her with stories told from her village in Zimbabwe. Her beautiful daughters and how proud she was of them. The tragedy of losing three sons. They laughed and they cried together. Angela was a shoulder to lean on.

Soon Servie and Angela crossed the bridge from a work relationship to a strong, deep friendship. Their bond blossomed into one of serving and loving each other. Two "sisters" born and raised thousands of miles apart. Two very different backgrounds. A beautiful and unlikely match. These two tender hearts wanted the best for each other. Grateful to have found each other. *"We all sing the same song,"* Servie thought.

CHAPTER 6

A Song of Service

"A life not lived for others is not a life."
Mother Teresa

Servie's eyes darted back and forth. Two piles of clothes and shoes neatly sorted before her on the bed. The smaller pile was hers. A couple of shirts and pants. An extra pair of shoes. And one dress for church. It was certainly enough.

She glanced at the second larger pile and smiled. Dozens of shirts and pants. And oh … all those ruffles and ribbons. Beautiful dresses for daughter Kimberly and more for the other little girls in the village. *Every girl deserves a dress.* And all those sandals. This was going to be a challenge. But she would find a way. If she had to connect them together and drape them around her neck, she would do it.

Servie thought about all those other children back in her village. Little brown feet finding their way to school. So many running through the village with no shoes. She could help them. *Every child needs a pair of shoes.* Servie wanted to make a difference.

It was the spring of 2012 and her annual trip back to Zimbabwe had arrived. A year of carefully checking and re-checking her figures to set aside money for that airline ticket. The counting had become an obsession of sorts. Counting money and time. Months, then weeks, then days. It was a focus that kept her going. A once-a-year chance to wrap her arms around those beautiful children of hers. And another opportunity to embrace her family and friends who were loving them for her.

She glanced again at the two piles before her and shook her head. One suitcase wasn't going to be enough. This was certainly going to be a two-suitcase trip. That was a good problem.

Servie had become a regular customer at the Goodwill Industries in town. Always looking for a deal. She visited the store often to browse through the children's section. It had become a mission to gather goods for all the children in the village.

Friends always cautioned her to focus inward.

"Servie you need to take care of yourself. Buy yourself something nice. A new dress. A new purse." Friends begged her to take care of herself.

But Servie couldn't do that. What about the others? How could she enjoy a new dress when others went without? It felt wrong.

And so, she chose to look outward. It diverted her attention from sorrow to sacrifice. It reinforced her purpose to provide. It gave her courage to feel again. And it made her heart happy.

. . .

There are so many kinds of sorrow and suffering. How many of us have suffered from infirmities of our mortal bodies, the sorrow caused from a separation by death, financial crises, loneliness, spiritual darkness, wayward children, disappointment … the list goes on. Situations we find ourselves in that hit hard and take our breath away. Cause us to lose hope.

Yet we are promised that our *"sorrow shall be turned to joy"* (John 16:20). How do we make that transition? We yearn for that assurance and emotional well-being during the most difficult journeys.

The answer comes not in an event, but through a process. Suffering tries and tests us. Suffering develops our spiritual strength. Suffering humbles and leads us to repentance. All leading to a spiritual anchor – faith in our Savior. Trials often give us the development of spirituality that we probably never would get if we didn't have the experience.

Again – how do we make that transition? One key path is that of service. Pulling our vision from plodding feet on a rocky, steep hill of circumstance to others. Lifting our eyes up to those around us. Taking some of the focus from our own feet and ministering to others whose feet plod their own difficult paths. It is an intentional focal point outside of our own turbulence. As we survive and endure, we must develop the ability to have a concern for others *while* we are suffering. It is key to our spiritual growth.

Jesus Christ gave us the perfect example in Gethsemane. He forgave His apostles who slept while he bled at every pore for all our sins. He only asked, *"could ye not watch with me one hour?"* (Matthew 26:40). Jesus Christ also expressed concern for His mother's care as He suffered great pain and anguish on the cross. And even while He was suffering, He taught the gospel to those who were suffering next to Him (see John 19:26-27).

Suffering is universal. How we react to suffering is individual. Suffering can take us one of two very different ways. It can be a strengthening and purifying experience combined with faith, or it can be a destructive force in our lives. If we have faith, we should be humbled and drawn to the Lord. If we do not have faith in the

Lord and His atoning sacrifice, there is added misery.[1]

Mother Teresa said, *"Prayer in action is love. Love in action is service."* To love and serve others is to emulate Jesus Christ. As we strive to live these principles – even and especially while suffering – we naturally draw closer to Him. Our relationship becomes tender and trusting. We feel a closeness. And there we find joy.

. . .

Servie's heart began to pound. The bus ride from the airport in Zimbabwe to her village seemed never-ending. The anticipation was both exhilarating and exhausting. Familiar streets grabbed her attention. Her fingers tightened on the handles of two large suitcases as the bus bumped along winding roads. Almost there.

Finally, the bus came to a stop and the doors opened. Servie stood and maneuvered the awkward bags toward the exit. She dragged each suitcase down the steps and off the bus. The heavy load had taken its toll. She wiped her brow with the back of her hand and smiled. Every bead of sweat worth it. Servie was home.

She looked up to see all eyes on her. Wide-eyed children and smiling adults had gathered. They knew she was coming. Several of the children threw their arms up in the air and cheered.

"Servie is here! Servie is here!"

They raced toward her and threw their arms around her waist. A few raced toward the village to alert the others. It was a homecoming celebration. Servie bent down and embraced each child taking in the joyous emotion. It felt so good to be here.

Servie lifted her eyes and searched for family. Saw them standing off to the side. They were shaking their heads and laughing. What a sight! Servie was gaining somewhat of a reputation in her village. Her sisters had jokingly began referring to her as the "Mother Teresa" of the village. Friends and neighbors knew she came bearing gifts. And they knew the gifts came out of love. Everyone felt that.

Servie ran over and wrapped her arms around family members and friends. Together they clung tight and wept with joy. It was a reunion better than any family picnic. Eyes told the story. They all shared and felt the heartaches of the past. But their hearts swelled for the goodness and wonder of a woman who seemed to rise above it all.

Servie turned toward the children who were dancing in the streets. They raced around like a swarm of bees waiting for direction from their queen.

"Come now! Help me with my bags. Let's see what I might have," she announced.

Servie took note of the two suitcases. One contained a small assembly of clothes for herself and dresses for her own daughter. She would open that later at the house. She unzipped the larger of the two suitcases and flung the top open. A treasure of clothes and shoes for the children on the streets who didn't have enough. Servie clapped her hands as though it was all a surprise to her.

"Look what we have here!" she exclaimed.

The children's eyes widened with excitement. Servie quickly surveyed the goods sorted before her and sized them up to the children who were gathered around. She held a dress up to a little girl.

"My, aren't you beautiful. What a princess you are."

The little girl clutched the dress and spun around believing Servie's pronouncement. Her eyes sparkled with glee. Perhaps she was.

The festivities continued. Dresses for little girls. Shirts and pants for playful little boys. And shoes to cover and protect those little bare feet.

Servie's mother watched the event unfold before her eyes. Oh, this daughter of hers. She was just different from the others. A heart too large for any chest to hold. Always giving. She was just like her father. The scene brought her back to earlier days when they all gathered together at the dinner table. A bowl of soup and bread. Suddenly, a knock at the door and a surprise visit from a neighbor. Servie's father was always the first to jump up and offer his plate.

"Have a seat. Come. We have soup for you," he would offer. He preferred to go without – always thinking of others. He would be proud of this daughter. This one definitely had his heart. She had seen that in Servie even as a young child.

"Hurry! Go walk with Servie to the bus stop," Servie's mother used to say. "Make sure she gets on that bus with the vegetables. Don't let her give everything away for free."

Fresh vegetables were plentiful in her village years ago when the children were little. Cabbage, corn, beans and peas. Bright orange carrots and leafy spinach. Mother would send Servie to ride the bus and sell to rural homes. Neighbors knew what was in those sacks. And neighbors knew that Servie was happy to share everything. How many times had Servie returned with empty sacks and no money. She simply wanted to give.

Mother shook her head and smiled at this festival of giving. Servie looked so happy. Nothing had changed. Vegetables then, and dresses now.

Precious days were spent catching up with friends and neighbors. Servie's trips lasted only two short weeks. There were joyful celebrations with family members. Servie's older daughters had traveled to back to Zimbabwe for the reunion. Servie had so much to share and in return wanted to hear all the details of happenings since her last visit. There were moments when it felt as though she had never left. Embraced by the beauty of these people and her surroundings, she tried to gather all the sights and sounds into her soul. Later she would revisit those emotions when she was thousands of miles away.

The time spent with her daughters was treasured. She clung to each moment. Holding tight to their smiles. Rejoicing in their happiness. And consuming the sensation of all daily adventures, whether trivial or significant. She breathed in their world – took a deep breath and held it all inside. Let it fill the empty chambers in her heart.

Servie felt a tender compassion for her little Kimberly. Just before this trip, Servie's brother had called to say that it was time to tell Kimberly the truth about her past. She was almost 14 years old now and deserved to know that this favorite "auntie" of hers that was coming back for another visit was really her mother. They discussed it and felt that he and his wife should be the first to explain things to her.

Servie's brother and wife had sat her down and gently explained. "We are all a family who supports each other," they said. "There are so many people who love you, Kimberly."

Kimberly nodded her head. She loved her family and felt happy. Servie's brother and wife gently continued.

"Your Auntie Servie is coming soon for another visit. She loves you so much, Kimberly. Together we have always helped each other in our family and there was a time when you were just 2 years old that Servie needed some help.

Kimberly's eyes widened. She had a funny feeling in her

stomach. She wanted to know more.

Together they talked about the tragedies of the past, the harsh reality of Servie not being able to provide for her children and why this "Auntie Servie" had to leave. They spoke of Servie's sacrifice in providing for her children. They looked directly at Kimberly.

"It was for *you*, Kimberly. She loves you that much. Honey … your mom is Servie. We promised her that we would love and care for you when she had to leave. We are one big family and we all love you. You have two moms, really."

It was a lot for a young girl to learn. These "siblings" that she had been raised with – they were really cousins. And those three cousins who died – they were her brothers.

They told Servie that Kimberly had cried with the new discovery. There were conflicting emotions which caused her to weep. Her young mind tried to sort through feelings and stories from the past. Kimberly had always had a strong connection with this "Auntie Servie." It was different and very real. Now she understood why.

Kimberly understood that everyone wanted to protect her – allow her to grow up in a family with no story attached. Just live as a happy child like everybody else. But above all Kimberly knew that she was loved. This family unit had always pulled together and Kimberly knew that would never change. Two moms – it helped to think of it that way. She knew that time would heal her emotions.

On the last day of her two-week visit, Servie went to visit Kimberly at the boarding school. She brought treats and small gifts. It was a thrill to see Kimberly doing so well in school. It confirmed all the hard work that Servie endured to pay for this education. She thought back to conversations with her husband years earlier. Together they promised to do whatever it took to give their children a fighting chance. They knew education was the key that unlocked a brighter future. Servie had lost her partner in this promised plan, but she would continue to fight alone to see it realized. Servie hugged her daughter goodbye.

"I'll see you on my next trip," Servie said.

Kimberly smiled. "Thank you, *Mom* ... for everything."

Servie's heart burned and she felt a wave of emotion. To hear Kimberly call her "mom" brought tears to her eyes. Oh, how she would miss this girl.

Servie dabbed at the corners of her eyes and walked down the corridor toward the classrooms. The headmaster at the school saw Servie speaking to one of the teachers. He smiled and walked up to greet her.

The headmaster's name was Easter. A fitting name for a kind, gentle man who worked with and loved the children at his school.

"I'm so glad you're here, Servie. I'd like to speak with you in my office," said Easter. "You have a minute?"

Servie followed him down the hall. She took a seat across from the desk. Easter looked at Servie. He knew of this woman's good heart.

"Servie, there's a girl here who is 13 years old. Her name is Sithabile. She just lost both parents. It's really tragic. They died of AIDS. We are all so concerned. Sithabile is left an orphan. I wondered if you might be able to help. We want her to stay here in school. She is so bright."

Servie considered what the headmaster was asking. She had never met the girl. Sithabile. It means "happiness." At this very moment, there surely was just hopelessness and despair in Sithabile's life. No happiness in sight. Servie knew where this path could lead. She had seen the devastating result of orphaned children on the streets, not only in her own village, but in other areas of Africa as well. She couldn't save the world, but perhaps she could save one child.

Servie looked across the desk at the headmaster and met his eyes. "I'll pay her fees. Keep the girl in school. I'll send the money as you need. I'll find a way."

Servie pondered the situation as she returned to her mother's home. Sithabile. She had never met the girl. Certainly, she would find a way to set aside money and help her find hope. Servie knew it was right. God would help her. What a devastating tragedy for a young girl to lose both parents. She would ask her mother to pray for Sithabile.

One final night of festivities and she would be returning back to Indiana. It had been a beautiful visit. Once again, her heart would ache as she thought about boarding the airplane again. She had taken this road so many times. God would help her do this hard thing. She trusted that. Tomorrow would be difficult. But within the darkness, her soul was filled with light. Servie felt it. And clung to that light.

. . .

What is charity? "*Charity suffereth long, and is kind; charity envieth not; charity vaunteth not itself, is not puffed up, doth not behave itself unseemly, seeketh not her own, is not easily provoked, thinketh no evil; rejoiceth not in iniquity, but rejoiceth in the truth; beareth all things, believeth all things, hopeth all things, endureth all things*" (1 Corinthians 13:4-7).

Since charity is the pure love of Christ, we should not be surprised to learn that Jesus embodied all the characteristics. He was the perfect example. The list of characteristics can appear overwhelming to us. In a world filled with distractions and despair, how can we exemplify all of these qualities? It can be a staggering thought.

Perhaps it is best to consider that charity is a process. What one thing can we do today that demonstrates this pure love of Christ? Tomorrow is another day. We try again and again to better ourselves. Soften our hearts. See others with His eyes. Over time that process changes our attitude. Suddenly we see life from a different perspective. It is a process of visualizing an eternal perspective when looking both inward and outward.

As we live the principle of charity, we open ourselves to a greater influence of the Spirit. Marion G. Romney said, "*No person whose soul is illuminated by the burning Spirit of God can in this world of sin and dense darkness remain passive. He is driven by an irresistible urge to fit himself to be an active agent of God in furthering righteousness ...* "[2]

It is a process of becoming more like Him – one simple charitable act at a time. Perhaps a measure of the level of our conversion to Jesus Christ is how we treat others. That one quality on the surface defines and exemplifies several of the characteristics in our definition of charity. It is a simple and telling analysis.

A life filled with charity is a life where joy and hope are found. Gandhi said, "*The best way to find yourself is to lose yourself in the service of others.*" Our selfish and woeful attention on our own struggles seems to lighten as we lift our heads and notice others. There is a direct connection between living a life of service and finding this hope and joy that we so earnestly seek.

The scriptures testify of this power. "*For whosoever will save his life shall lose it; but whosoever shall lose his life for my sake and the gospel's, the same shall save it"* (Mark 8:35). Here the Savior is telling us that unless we lose ourselves in service to others, there is little purpose to our own lives. If we live only for ourselves, we eventually shrivel up and *lose our lives.* In contrast, if we lose ourselves in service to others, we grow and flourish. In effect, we are saving our lives.[3]

We may feel unhappy in current circumstances. But it is possible to feel unhappy in our present, mortal situation and still have joy. How? Because joy has a spiritual aspect to it. Finding an adequate definition of joy in several dictionary sources does not quite match the mark from our perspective. We find dictionary descriptions of joy as a feeling of happiness or contentment that comes from success, good fortune, or a sense of well-being. Examples include words like pleasure, fun and gratification.

The scriptures use a phrase – *a fulness of joy* – that provides greater clarity and useful insights. For example, in Psalms we read, "*In thy presence* (meaning the Lord's) *is fulness of joy"* (Psalm 16:11). This definition of the *fulness of joy*, then, is being in the presence of the Father and the Son and the promise of the scriptures to us is that we were created to be able to return to them and experience this *fulness of joy*. Fundamental to the entire plan of salvation is that we might achieve joy – real joy. Clearly, then, joy means more to us than momentary comfort.[4]

Despite what is happening in our surroundings, we can find joy based on this higher definition. Gordon B. Hinckley said, "*My plea is if we want joy in our hearts, if we want the Spirit of the Lord in our lives, let us forget ourselves and reach out. Let us put in the background our own personal, selfish interests and reach out in service to others. In so doing, we will find the truth of the Master's great promise of glad tidings.*"[5]

A joyful heart is a charitable heart. A joyful heart sees eternity in perspective. And a joyful heart sings.

. . .

Servie rose with the Indiana sun the day after returning from her trip back home. She was eager to start the day and spend it with Angela. What a wonderful friend she had become. Working for her was wonderful. It hardly seemed fair to accept wages for household duties in such a friendly environment. And when Angela was in town – even better. They could spend hours together.

Servie caught Angela up on all the stories from her recent visit to Zimbabwe. Not a single detail was spared. The family, all the happenings in her village and all those children. Servie tried to find the words to describe the joy at distributing the clothing to those in need. Angela could see it in Servie's face. Moist eyes as she recounted the village children running here and there. A celebration. Hugs for all.

And then there was Sithebile. A new tender connection for Servie. She spoke as if Sithebile were her adopted daughter. Servie's shattered heart had reached out and pulled this new orphan into her life. Sithebile's school fees were not a burden. Servie spoke of it as an opportunity. A privilege to give back. This young girl wanted to grow up to be a teacher. Servie was determined to make that happen.

"Oh, Angela, I met some people who want to build an orphanage in the village to help the children who live on the street," Servie exclaimed. "They are in such need. I want to do more. I want to help them build a new place for the children. A place that is close enough that the children can walk to school. I will send money. These children need a nice place with teachers and people to care for them."

Servie's eyes were big and encouraged as she spoke of a future dream. "Maybe one day they will plant a garden. I can give them my cows for milk. Maybe one day it will get finished and I will be one of the happiest people in the world. I will go and visit them every year. And they will grow up knowing that I loved them. They will know that I did something for them."

Angela sat back and smiled, witnessing the transformation occurring. This friend who had been through so much, yet finding a way to nurture another … and another. To open up her heart. This humble woman before her always reaching out. It was beautiful to behold.

"What do you hear from your lawyer?" Angela asked.

Servie shook her head. "He says it's complicated. I gave him more money. He says there are still roadblocks and he is trying to find a way to bring Kimberly here to the United States. Maybe he will find a way very soon."

Angela considered the situation. This lawyer had been working on this issue for too many years. Angela's gut told her something was not right. There were no solid answers and too much time. Surely there was a better way.

"The next time you go meet with your lawyer, let me go with you," Angela said.

"Okay," Servie replied. "I see him Monday morning."

Angela made a mental note. She would rearrange her schedule to meet Servie's lawyer. She would wear her formal hat and attire just to make a little different impression. Angela wanted to ensure that this lawyer knew expectations were being made, and to ensure that she would be following up with him.

Servie's other daughters were doing well. They were now living outside the harsh realities of Zimbabwe. They had been able to take advantage of educational programs and were thriving in their blossoming new careers in the UK. Servie's extended family had really wrapped their arms around these children and provided shelter for their education and growth. Angela hoped she would meet them all someday. But this little Kimberly – Servie's little number six, now already fourteen. The hope of her leaving Zimbabwe and joining Servie here in the United States was fading. Too many years had passed. This candle of hope was barely flickering.

But Servie would never give up. Perhaps the flame was dim, but it was still alive. Servie still had a song within her heart. A song of hope.

. . .

What is the test? To endure to the end with clenched fists and gritted teeth? To curl up and pray away our circumstance and wait on the Lord? No – a higher commitment is expected. The real challenge and test in this mortal life is to reach outward while the storms rage within us. The tendency is to recoil. Focus inward. But while a charitable heart serves another, the selfless process softens our own heart. A soft heart is more receptive and open to a deeper relationship with the Lord. As we serve in healing others, He heals us.

The true challenge of our lives is to become more like the Savior. No single act, deed, or experience will make us a good or respectable person. But a lifetime of events forms our character. Change us for the better. We become more and more like Him. The result is feelings of joy resulting from an accumulation of deeds and attitudes. Joy – despite difficulties surrounding us.[6]

It was once said by an unknown poet –

Live so that those who know you
And don't know Him
Will want to know Him
Because they know you.

Our character is defined through words, actions and deeds. While we quietly serve others, our countenance shines. This countenance reflects the pure love of Christ. And it is noticed.

Service can begin with a single, simple act. Thomas S. Monson taught, "*Often small acts of service are all that is required to lift and bless another: a question concerning a person's family, quick words of encouragement, a sincere compliment, a small note of thanks, a brief telephone call. If we are observant and aware, and if we act on the promptings which come to us, we can accomplish much good.*"[7]

Too often we can talk ourselves out of a good deed. Dark periods in our own lives and overflowing to-do lists on daily agendas complicate our lives. It is easy to get into a routine where those lists become so important that opportunities to serve outside of that list are unnoticed. This tunnel vision with focus on "the list" prevent us from seeing others around us. We blindly live side by side but do not communicate heart to heart. Their hands are outstretched, but we choose not to see.

Certainly, as good people, we *intend* to serve and help those in need. We recognize that our hearts have been touched as we have witnessed the need of another. Often, we have *intended* to be the one to help, but then left it for others thinking surely someone will take care of that need. We become so caught up in the busyness of our own lives. Sometimes there is a need to step back and take a good look. We may find that we have immersed ourselves in the "thick of thin things" – taking care of things which do not really matter much at all in the grand scheme.

As we lift our heads and use spiritual eyes to see, we will notice that we are surrounded by those in need to our attention, our encouragement, our support, our comfort, and our kindness. They may be family members, friends, acquaintances, or strangers. We are commanded to serve and lift His children. The Lord is dependent upon each of us.[8]

Sometimes we feel prompted to reach beyond our comfort zone. To serve and love those outside our social or economic circles. Mother Teresa said, *"The most terrible poverty is loneliness and the feeling of being unloved."* She was a beautiful example of serving and loving as He would. She was a light in very dark places. In the New Testament, we read in the book of Matthew about those who are the *"hungred … thirsty … naked … sick …"* and Jesus Christ reminds us that *"Inasmuch as ye have done it unto one of the least of these my brethren, ye have done it unto me"* (Matthew 25:35-40).

It is recognizing that there are others who suffer, perhaps more, than we do in our current situation. That perspective opens eyes and hearts. Soon we cannot help but be drawn to help with hearts full of charity and love. Once we understand that we are all here as brothers and sisters of a Father in Heaven, it is easier to break through walls of differences. With understanding we appreciate that all of us are on the same mortal mission. There is a spiritual connection. We become one with those we serve. And one with Him.

There is a World War II story told about a large statue of Jesus Christ which was severely damaged in the bombing of a city. When the townspeople found the statue among the rubble, they mourned because it had been a beloved symbol of their faith. A symbol of God's presence in their lives. Most of the statue was repaired by experts, but its hands had been damaged so severely that they could not be restored. A sculptor could have been hired to make new hands, but they decided to leave it as it was – a permanent reminder of the tragedy of war. A statue without hands. The people of the city added a sign to the base of the statue which contained these words: "You are my hands."[9]

Like the Savior, we have hands outstretched, hands reaching out to comfort, heal, bless and love. He loved the humble and the meek and walked among them wherever He walked. He ministered. And He offered hope and salvation.

If our hands are His, they must be stretched out in compassion toward others, for everyone is walking his or her own difficult path. It can be easy to condemn or wonder how they got themselves in this poor condition. That perhaps they deserve their suffering for choices they have made. But it is unworthy of us as Christians to think that those who suffer deserve their suffering. In Proverbs, we read that "*a friend loveth at all times, and a brother is born for adversity*" (Proverbs 17:17). We must love at all times – including when our brothers and sisters suffer during times of adversity.

Charity is about action, not just words. Songs and poems can speak of love all day long, but until we manifest that love in action, our words are empty. Christ served and showed his love each day of His life. Even in the midst of the crowd, He still noticed and reached out to the one.

As we become Christ's hands and extend them and our hearts toward others, something wonderful happens to us. Our own spirits become healed. We become refined. Stronger. We become happier and find peace and hope in our own lives. A softer heart is more receptive to the whisperings of the Holy Spirit. We are changed.[10]

This transformation comes over time when we serve as His hands. Eyes now see others in a new light as brothers and sisters in need. Ears hear the Spirit whisper and we are compelled to act. And a voice now sings a new song. A song of love. A song of hope. A song of service.

CHAPTER 7

Then Sings My Soul

"Launch out into the deep, and your nets will be filled."
Joseph Smith

"Mom! It's so good to hear your voice."

It was Sithabile. Servie's heart swelled as she heard this sweet girl's voice over the phone. A beautiful girl orphaned by parents who died of AIDS years ago and who Servie now loved as one of her own. Sithabile was clearly excited to share some good news.

Servie smiled. Bringing this girl into her life was one of the best decisions she had ever made. This girl was bright. She had qualified for an exchange program to serve in an orphanage program over in Bolivia and was eager to help Servie build her dream. An orphanage for children running the streets in their village. It was the start of 2014 and the air was filled with hope for the future. Both Servie and Sithabile felt it.

When Servie flew back for annual visits to Zimbabwe, she brought Sithabile into her family's home and loved her. The whole extended family had also adopted her into their loving circle. Servie knew that she was both mom and dad to Sithabile. She was all this girl had in the world. School supplies, uniforms and fees were paid to ensure Sithabile could continue past high school on her path to be a teacher. Not just any teacher. One who felt a deep sense of rescue. She hoped to teach the orphaned children and give them a fighting chance. A chance like Servie had given her.

"Mom, I have found 10 kids who are orphans. They really need our help."

Her enthusiasm was contagious. Servie smiled as she listened to tender descriptions of each child and their needs. Sithabile was filled with hope that they could somehow make a difference. These two were both strong women whose hearts wanted to save the world. And they wanted to save it now.

"I'll send some more money for the construction," Servie said. "For bags of cement."

Servie had found a group in Zimbabwe who wanted to help build something to house the orphaned children living on the streets in her village. They were ready and willing, but they needed more funding. Servie sacrificed to send whatever she could to support the cause. One day she hoped Sithabile could run the place and that thought made Servie's heart soar.

But construction in Zimbabwe was slow. Planning and organization was subpar. And financial dishonesty was rampant. Servie wouldn't send money for such a project to just anybody, but she trusted some project leaders in the village and she trusted Sithabile. This young orphaned woman had replaced a hole in her heart.

Servie hung up the phone and smiled. She admired Sithabile's determination and positive energy. A once quiet, reserved child who had risen from the ashes wanting to do great things. Wanting to make a difference.

. . .

Servie rushed up the front walk to Angela's house. She was so excited to see her. Angela had been traveling quite a bit lately and returned home late the night before. Servie managed affairs and took care of everything Angela needed at the house, but she had missed her company. The two had become the best of friends. Always looking out for each other.

Servie let herself in and found Angela in the kitchen. She embraced her and they sat for a bit to catch up on everything in their lives. It felt so good to be with Angela. She was warm and kind and genuinely interested in Servie. There was a strong bond between these two. Servie knew in her heart that this friendship was different.

Angela leaned back in her chair and looked at her friend – considered what she had been through. She paused for a moment then looked directly at Servie.

"I have a question – a proposal really," Angela said. "Something I'd like you to consider."

Servie met Angela's gaze. She leaned forward giving her full attention.

"You know I have the home in Arizona and a smaller guest house. It's beautiful there. Different than it is here. High desert and cactus instead of all this green. Wonderfully warm in the winter. We don't even have a snow shovel there. No need for one. I'm back and forth all the time. And on my last visit I decided it needs some work. I need some help managing the affairs there. What would you think about moving to Arizona with me? I'd go back and forth as I always have. Continue to travel for work. But that could be your new home. I would help you get settled."

Servie's eyes widened as she considered the request. Angela noticed.

"Just think about it," Angela said.

Servie thought hard for about two seconds.

"I'd love to," she said. "Absolutely."

There was no doubt in Servie's mind that she would follow her friend. It didn't even feel like work when she was with Angela. It was more like serving her friend. Together they would continue to work in Arizona on getting Kimberly into the United States. It somehow felt so right.

Servie's friends felt differently. Friends from her previous job and her neighborhood loved Servie and didn't want to see her go.

"Everything is going well for you Servie," they said. "We don't think you should go."

But Servie recognized the feeling in her heart. A voice inside. It told her differently. There were many justified reasons why she should stay in Indiana. Those reasons made sense. Her friends meant well. But Servie felt a sense of peace that quieted all the arguments. She would follow what her heart was whispering.

Servie began to make plans for the move.

. . .

Servie's phone lit up. A call was coming in. The number was from Zimbabwe. She let it ring. Phone calls from Zimbabwe could not be answered. The anxiety from just seeing the country code caused Servie's heart to pound. Friends and family in Zimbabwe knew they must leave a message. Too many phone calls had delivered devastating news. Servie had made herself a promise. A sort of survival tactic. No answering phone calls from Zimbabwe. Everyone there knew to leave a message. "No worries," they would say. "There is no bad news, Servie. Just call us back."

Servie watched the phone and heard the familiar sound as a voicemail was left. It always took some courage just to listen to that. Often Servie would let hours pass before she could check. In a strange way, the phone had become the enemy.

Servie took a deep breath and picked up the phone. She looked closely at the number and recognized it immediately. It was Easter, the headmaster at the boarding school. He must be calling about Kimberly. She pushed the buttons to hear the voicemail.

"Servie, it's Easter. I'm afraid I don't have good news. It's Sithabile. She's at the hospital with a very bad headache. She's had it for a couple of days and it is worse. We are hoping the doctors can help her. I will call you when I know more. We are praying for her Servie."

Servie felt the familiar pain travel from her stomach up into her heart. "*Not again,*" she thought. "*I can't do this again.*"

It was late. She had spent the day packing things up and getting organized for the move to Arizona. Both her body and mind were tired. Servie sat on the edge of the bed and stared at the device. She hated that phone. She picked it up and carried it into the kitchen, placed it on the counter behind the potted plant and returned to her bedroom. A deliberate and desperate action. She refused to allow this conversation to continue tonight.

Servie buried her head into her pillow and pulled the sides up around her face as if to cushion her mind from the world. She curled up into a ball and let the soft fabric on her pillow absorb her tears. "*Just go to sleep. Tomorrow will be better.*" Servie begged the negative thoughts to stop and willed herself to find sleep. Sleep would stop the endless torment. Stop the what-ifs.

But sleep would not win this battle. It was an endless night. Long and dark and anything but restful. A glimmer of light peaked through the bedroom window. The night had finally surrendered to the first rays of sunlight on the horizon.

Servie sat up in bed and rubbed her weary eyes. Angela was expecting her today. Maybe a hot shower would deliver some needed energy. Servie made a mental note about getting some extra sleep the following night.

Servie quickly dressed then grabbed her purse and coat and stopped by the kitchen sink for a much-needed drink of water. She gulped it down, anxious to get on her way. This morning she would skip breakfast. The pit in her stomach would not allow food to enter. As she set the glass in the sink she noticed the phone behind the plant.

The dreaded enemy. She stood very still. Daring herself to pick it up and place it inside her purse.

Suddenly it lit up. Servie jumped at the sight. She peaked around the pot to see the number. It belonged to the headmaster.

Servie pulled the kitchen chair close and sat down hard. She gripped the edge of the counter tight as the room began to spin. She put her head down and tried to breathe deeply. This was ridiculous. Perhaps it was good news. She needed to listen to the message. Surely it was an update on Sithabile.

Servie pulled the phone up to her ear. She pushed the voicemail button.

"Servie, it's Easter. I'm so sorry. She ... she died, Servie. The doctors couldn't save Sithabile. They say it was meningitis. Call me back, Servie. I'm so sorry."

Servie was startled by a loud wailing noise then realized it was coming from somewhere deep within her chest. A harrowing cry from the darkest depths of despair. Servie knew this place intimately – a place that she had visited too many times. Not another child. How many times could her heart break?

Servie lay on the kitchen floor. Not quite remembering how she got there. She curled up on the hard surface and pulled her knees in tight. She brought her coat up around her neck and sobbed.

. . .

Angela wrapped her arms around her grieving friend. She had listened with her heart and cried with Servie. How much more could this beautiful friend take?

Angela had never met anybody with a more tender, caring heart. This grieving woman wanted to love and save the world one child at a time. But in the last few years, she had lost again and again. Servie's eyes were hollow and dark. The grief was etched on her face. That beautiful smile was gone.

For the first time, Servie had shown real signs of losing hope.

"Why?" Servie cried. "Why is this happening?"

There were no answers. And the grief had magnified Servie's desire to bring Kimberly to the United States. But the glimmer of hope was gone. It was all just too hard.

Angela knew what Servie needed to hear.

"Let's continue to make a plan for Arizona," said Angela. "Go to the sunshine. I'll help you get settled and we'll figure things out. We'll find a way to bring Kimberly to Arizona."

Both Angela and Servie knew that this change of scenery was best. A new start for Servie. A busy mind with new responsibilities managing affairs for Angela at the Arizona house. The timing was perfect.

. . .

Where is hope? At times, it feels so very far away. All we feel is discouragement, emptiness, sadness, disappointment and despair. Questions of why and how plague our thoughts. It is difficult to see beyond the struggle and at our lowest points cannot even wonder what we are to learn. We feel physically, emotionally and spiritually beaten.

But there is hope. There is always hope. Where do we find it? An immediate turnaround of events which will eliminate the issue? Not likely. A removal of stress and strife in our current situation? Hardly.

Hope is an eternal principle and is often a long-range perspective in its true form. It is lifting our head and looking beyond present circumstances. It is looking up to promised eternal blessings. It is trusting that God's word is sincere and perfect.

Scriptures teach that we knew the plan before we came here. We fully understood its dimension and promise. We were spirits eager to gain a mortal body and the ability to *feel*. We knew there would be joy. And we knew there would be struggles. The opportunity was presented to learn through this mortal experience and we eagerly chose the plan understanding that it was set up for success. The Holy Ghost to guide and the Savior to save. We would not be alone. There was no doubt.

This is a plan of hope, and we have a perfect example to follow. The Savior's life and teachings that he left for us are perfect patterns. Following them and adopting them as our own patterns pulls us closer to Him.

The Savior faced and felt heartache similar to those we experience. And he handled each situation in a perfect manner.

In the Garden of Gethsemane he felt it all – pain, discouragement, disappointment, loneliness. It is through His atonement that we are given the power to do hard things, the assurance that we are not alone, and the possibility to obtain salvation.

If only we had spiritual eyes to see the paths being cleared. Quiet nudges toward direction in our lives. Perhaps new and different paths than we had ever thought. In the darkest of nights, our Savior is lighting the way. We must position our heart and mind to see His light, to hear words which direct and to feel His comfort.

In Matthew 11:28-29 we read:

"Come unto me, all ye that labour and are heavy laden, and I will give you rest. Take my yoke upon you, and learn of me; for I am meek and lowly in heart: and ye shall find rest unto your souls."

He lives. He loves. And He knows.

. . .

Servie leaned back in her chair and tilted her head back. She closed her eyes and felt the warm rays of sunshine on her face. It fed her soul.

The Arizona desert was beautiful in a different kind of way. Rugged landscape and boulders mixed with creosote bushes, palo verde trees and cholla cactus. The saguaro cacti stood tall and majestic with arms reaching for the sky in this rugged landscape. Birds she had never heard before sang their songs. It was alive. A slight breeze cooled her neck.

This felt right. This strange new environment was where she belonged. A quiet voice inside had led her here. She had learned to trust that voice. There was a healing energy here. She could feel it making a difference.

Angela had helped Servie move into the Arizona house and get everything settled. There was so much to learn here, but Servie was eager for the challenge. She opened her eyes and surveyed the landscape. How would she grow anything in this? She missed her vegetable garden and would need to learn new ways of gardening in this hot, dry climate. One day she would conquer that.

She heard Angela calling from the other room.

"Servie, are you ready?"

Servie walked back inside to the mirror by the front door and positioned the beautiful white hat on her head. It had been a gift from Angela. They were both dressed in their Sunday best.

"Yes. Let's go!" Servie replied.

They were headed to the Catholic church for Sunday services. Angela had been born and raised in the Catholic religion and she had found this place of worship shortly after the move. Servie was excited to attend with her friend. She loved their time together.

Servie sat on the bench and listened to the pastor. He seemed nice enough. He loved God and taught inspiring messages from the Bible. The room was large and full. Not a single empty bench. So many people. Too many people. This was different from the small church in Zimbabwe where her mother had brought Servie each Sunday as a child. Different from the village church where Servie had also brought her own children years later. She felt disconnected. Something was missing.

The two friends left the services and made the decision to drive around town. It was worth looking at some housing in the area. At some point Servie might want to get her own place and make the guest house available for Angela's family.

They made a left turn and headed down a street that looked promising. There was a new development of townhomes on the left. But that's not what caught Servie's attention. There was a church on the other side of the street. Smaller than the Catholic church, but beautiful in a simple way. It had a steeple that pointed to the heavens and a sign out front that said The Church of Jesus Christ of Latter-day Saints.

Servie felt a flutter in her gut.

"I want to try that church," she said to Angela and pointed across the street. "I want to try this one next week."

"Okay," replied Angela. "You can drive my other car here and I'll drive separately to mine."

. . .

Servie walked up the sidewalk leading to the main doors of the new church. There was no movement in the parking lot behind her. Servie was alone in this decision. But she wanted to follow that small feeling. She was curious about this church, hopeful that she would feel a connection.

Servie opened the door and immediately saw a chapel off the lobby. She peaked her head in the door and saw a room filled with families. She quietly entered and took a seat toward the back of the room. The service was already in progress.

Servie's eyes darted back and forth across the congregation. She pondered what she saw. "*I may have made a mistake. There is nobody like me. Am I really going to be comfortable here?*" The people speaking at the microphone were sincere and happy. They talked about their relationship and understanding of God. There were many words that Servie didn't comprehend, but she liked the way she felt. There was peace here.

The congregation joined together in song and then a

final prayer was given. Servie gathered up her purse and Bible and glanced at her watch to check the time. She looked up to a kind smiling face. It was the same man who had talked at the microphone earlier. He introduced himself as the bishop.

One by one people gathered to welcome Servie and introduce themselves. It became a receiving line of sorts. Men and women gathered to meet this new visitor in their midst. They were truly welcoming and genuinely happy to see her. They smiled and shook her hand over and over again. It was amazing.

Servie drove home and considered what she had just felt.

"How was it?" Angela said.

"Oh, Angela! I found the right church!"

"Why?" Angela replied.

"All the people I met were very kind. So, so kind. People were running to meet me. The bishop was so nice," Servie said. Her eyes were bright again. That big smile had returned.

Angela had attended an open house at a new temple in Gilbert months ago. She learned that when faithful members of The Church of Jesus Christ of Latter-day Saints attend temples, they find opportunities for peaceful reflection and learn more about God's plan of happiness. Members could also be married in temples for time and eternity, as well as bless and serve those who've gone before them through ordinances. They believe that every person who has lived on the earth is entitled to the opportunity to receive the blessings of eternal life. The building was impressive and the people were gracious. Angela understood the members gathered in the meetinghouses, such as this one, for their weekly worship services. She was curious.

Angela had learned very recently that her mother had been a member of this church. A small detail only learned in a discussion following the death of her aunt. Members of this aunt's church had served and cared for the family following her death. Angela saw incredible love and sacrifice as these church members embraced what needed to be done with tender condolences, dinners, and help with packing.

Angela pondered the full circle. Her own mother born and raised in this church of Jesus Christ. But because her mother married someone who was Catholic, they raised their children in that faith. Angela hadn't known any differently. Now, after that recent revelation of family history and the tour of this beautiful temple, Angela wanted to know more. Months ago, she filled out an information card at the temple and planned to attend a Sunday service soon.

Angela smiled at her friend's happiness. It was nice to see Servie's face all lit up. Perhaps she would try attending once just to see what this was all about.

. . .

Servie took a deep breath and blew it out slowly. She reached up and rubbed her forehead. The lawyer had called to say that he was completing the paperwork and would be submitting it to immigration. Nobody understood why it was taking so long. There was nothing more he could do. He encouraged Servie to be patient.

Be patient? For how many years! This went way beyond patience.

Servie had called to talk to her two older daughters earlier that day. She was so proud of them. Both Thandeka and Thembelihle had finished their college work and were now establishing careers. Thandeka was still living in the UK and

Thembelihle was now living in Australia. Servie thought back to earlier times after her husband had died. How she loved her family for helping her to raise and educate these two bright girls. Servie felt as though her sacrifice was not forgotten when talking to these two. To see the success and hear their happy voices over the phone made it all worthwhile. Servie's heart soared when she thought of all they had accomplished.

But there was still Kimberly. Her little one. Born so tiny and frail that nobody had expected her to live. Yet she had thrived. Servie remembered back to that first long walk onto the airplane fourteen years ago. A desperate look back at 2-year-old Kimberly in the arms of her brother and sister-in-law. An emotional torture wrestling with dreams of providing food and education for six children. Had the sacrifices been worth it? She questioned that now. Servie's family had scooped Kimberly up as their own and loved her. But Servie had missed so much of this little one's life. Too much …

If the governments would just approve her passport. If only Kimberly could attend high school here in Arizona. Mother and daughter together under the same roof. Then scholarships for college. It was Servie's dream for her daughter.

Patience? That ran out long ago. Servie's mother had always taught her children never to give up hope. That God would provide a way. Servie needed her mother's belief and optimism. She needed her mother's prayers. And she needed her mother's faith. Servie's flame of hope was barely lit.

. . .

Servie looked at herself in the mirror and smiled. She admired

120

the dress that Angela had purchased for her. And the hat was the perfect touch. Something Servie would never have done for herself. She felt beautiful and happy. Excited this Sunday morning to share this new adventure with her best friend.

Angela walked into the living room. Her dress, hat and shoes all worked together like a beautifully framed piece of art. It was a bright, sunny day. A perfect day to celebrate friendship and God. She and Servie would try attending this new church.

Together these two walked into the chapel, marched right up to the front and took a seat centered in front of the pulpit. Their outfits were spectacular. Heads turned as they made their way to the chosen spot. Two sisters – one white and one black. Both donning fabulous hats to celebrate the occasion.

Following the services, the bishop quickly made his way over to them.

"Hello again," he said. "So nice to see you."

Together they greeted the bishop. He quickly made a connection between where they lived and another family who attended there. It turned out they were neighbors. Introductions were made and friendships formed. Once again, this congregation swarmed the two women and welcomed them to their place of worship. Servie beamed as she witnessed the same interest and kindness felt a week earlier. Her eyes met Angela's. These were such warm, happy people. She could see that Angela felt it, too. Once again, Servie felt peace in this place.

The bishop introduced two young women to Servie and Angela. They were missionaries here for a time to teach. They invited Servie and Angela to a family history lesson they were giving in the next hour. Angela had always had an interest in genealogy.

"Sure, we'd love to," they said and followed the two into a classroom.

Discussions went from personal backgrounds and why these two bright, young women would serve a mission away from home, to family history and the principle of eternal families. The spirit was strong and there was a genuine interest in learning more. Angela and Servie eagerly agreed to have the missionaries come to their home and teach them more. An appointment was made for later that week.

That afternoon, Servie heard the doorbell. Two young boys stood smiling at the door. She recognized them as children from the family at church that the bishop had introduced as neighbors.

"We'd love to help with your garbage cans," they said. "It's a long way down the hill to where the garbage truck picks up. You don't need to pull yours down there and back every week. We're happy to do that for you."

Servie hugged the boys and thanked them for their generous offer. It was incredible. Servie shook her head as she closed the door behind them. What kind, wonderful people. "*They don't even know me.*" The offer meant more than these boys knew.

. . .

Servie sat quietly with her Bible in her lap. She listened carefully as the two missionaries taught her about God, taught that He was a part of our eternal family, taught that He was approachable, and that prayer was a way to talk to Him.

Servie had never prayed by herself. That was something that her mother always did for the family. With this new understanding of who God was, she wanted to try. The missionaries helped her.

"Dear God," Servie started. She practiced with the missionaries. They helped her speak from her heart and taught her that He was listening.

Later lessons focused on the plan of salvation and Joseph Smith's vision. There was so much to learn. It all made sense. Servie pondered everything taught. She read from her Bible each day and also the Book of Mormon that the missionaries had given her. Servie understood now that God was her Heavenly Father. A name that she had never heard before. She began to address him with the new name in prayer.

"Dear Heavenly Father," she would whisper.

The name better described a new closeness she felt with Him. It described Him as part of this eternal family that she was learning about. It became easier and more comfortable to pray. She talked to her Heavenly Father and asked for help – help with heartache, depression and hope. Servie also understood that she needed to forgive. She had seen some terrible things in her life: the war in her village and her son's murderer. She would never forget, but she wanted to forgive. She wanted to turn it over to Him.

Servie loved what she was learning. Every day she pulled her scriptures onto her lap and read. She studied the messages. What once had just been black and white words now seemed to come alive.

During one particular lesson with the missionaries, they asked Servie if she had any questions. She had been particularly quiet. The missionaries could see she was reflecting on all these new principles.

Servie nodded her head. She loved these young women. They were sensitive, considerate and so willing to help.

"I have three sons," she said quietly. "All three have died. I miss them every day. There is not a day that goes by that I don't think about each one of them. Not a single day."

Servie paused and felt a wave of emotion.

"You teach about eternal families. This plan where we will all be together again after this life."

The missionaries didn't rush her. They nodded and let her continue.

"Will I see my boys again?"

"Yes, you will Servie. That is part of the beautiful plan. This life is not the end. The Savior has made that possible."

Servie felt a burning in her heart. She felt at peace. This new understanding gave her hope. It broke down walls of torment and despair that were buried deep within her heart. A new eternal perspective that changed everything. Nothing could reverse what had happened in the past, but suddenly there was hope for a future reunion with her three precious boys. Sweet Sithabile. Her husband. Her father.

It made sense. She didn't have all the answers, but God would help her. She felt Him closer than ever in her life. She would never be alone.

Servie felt the voice inside again.

"I want to belong to this church," Servie said. "I'd like to be baptized."

. . .

Spencer W. Kimball said: "*Our great need, and our great calling, is to bring to the people of this world the candle of understanding to light their way out of obscurity and darkness and into the joy, peace, and truths of the gospel*"[1]

Why would young men and women give up two vital years of their life to teach? It is a calling. It is about passion and testimony. And it is a desire to share that personal knowledge with the world. It brings such joy and happiness and it changes lives. Once felt, the eagerness to share it with others exceeds the perceived sacrifice.

Missionary work is a life calling. If you're old enough to be a member of the church, you're old enough to be a missionary. It is about sharing the light and hope that gives meaning to this life.

The darkness of death and despair can be dispelled by the light of revealed truth.

"I am the resurrection, and the life:" Jesus Christ said, *"… he that believeth in me, though he were dead, yet shall he live: And whosoever liveth and believeth in me shall never die …"* (John 11:25-26).

This reassurance and holy confirmation of life beyond the grave could well be the peace promised by the Savior when He assured his disciples: *"Peace I leave with you, my peace I give unto you: not as the world giveth, give I unto you. Let not your heart be troubled, neither let it be afraid"* (John 14:27).

Thomas S. Monson said, *"This is the knowledge that sustains. This is the truth that comforts. This is the assurance that guides those bowed down with grief out of the shadows and into the light. Such help is not restricted to the elderly, the well-educated, or a select few. It is available to all."*[2]

This hope that we are given by the resurrection is our conviction that death is not the conclusion of our identity, but merely a necessary step in the destined transition from mortality to immortality. This hope changes our whole perspective of mortal life. It gives us strength to endure the mortal challenges faced by each of us and by those we love. We know that physical, mental, or emotional deficiencies we bring with us at birth or acquire during mortal life are only temporary.

This assurance and hope helps us understand that the resurrection will include an opportunity to be with our family members – husband, wife, parents, brothers and sisters, children, and grandchildren. It is a powerful encouragement for us to love and fulfill our family responsibilities in mortality and anticipate joyful reunions in the next.[3]

Ultimately, our acceptance of Him and his influence is up to us. The Lord's hand is outstretched to every individual. We must look for it. Where do we find it? In chapels? In holy temples? The answer is yes. And, also perhaps, where you would least expect. He extends His hand in the lowest of places. Death, nor despair, nor devastation can sink lower than He did in the Garden of Gethsemane. He felt all – so He could comfort all.

Isaiah foretold, "*He will swallow up death in victory; and the Lord God will wipe away tears from off all faces; and the rebuke of his people shall he take away from off all the earth: for the Lord hath spoken it*" (Isaiah 25:8).

Each of us has the opportunity to know these truths for ourselves. We each have our own agency. It takes some work, some effort and an open heart. Joseph Smith said:

"*Search the scriptures – search the revelations which we publish, and ask your Heavenly Father, in the name of His Son Jesus Christ, to manifest the truth unto you, and if you do it with an eye single to His glory, nothing doubting, He will answer you by the power of His Holy Spirit. You will then know for yourselves and not for another. You will not then be dependent on man for the knowledge of God.*"[4]

CHAPTER 8

One Song

"I wait for the Lord, my soul doth wait,
and in his word do I hope."
Psalms 130:5

Servie smiled and grabbed Angela's hand. Two women filled
with joy on this special occasion. Servie was dressed in white. Her
very best friend seated next to her. The room was overflowing
with friends from church. A beautiful spirit filled the room. One of
friendship, love and reverence. Servie's smile reflected what she felt
inside.

Angela had also spent many days with the missionaries
learning more about this new church. Her heart was touched and
she embraced the gospel. Her husband and daughter respected
and supported this decision that she felt so strongly about. Angela
had been baptized a week ago and was now here to support Servie.

Angela took her place at the podium in the front of the room
where the baptism would take place. She had been asked to give a
few remarks. Angela looked at Servie and smiled. Then she began
to speak. Servie's eyes widened. It couldn't be! Angela was speaking
in the language of Zulu. It was a tribute from Angela to Servie.
Angela had contacted Servie's sister and requested the translation
of her remarks from English into Zulu. She had practiced the

foreign pronunciation over and over. Those in attendance felt it. The spirit was strong.

Two sisters. One black. One white. Together singing one song.

Servie felt like she had come home: a new home of understanding, a new home of peace and belonging.

Servie walked up to the baptismal font. She was helped into the water by a smiling young man who months before had offered to pull the garbage cans for Servie. He was just getting ready to serve a two-year mission of his own. But before he left, Servie would be his first baptism.

. . .

Three missionaries pulled up to the front of Servie's home. They were excited to spend a few minutes teaching more about the gospel. Servie was eager to learn and they were just as eager to teach.

They pulled up the steep driveway and could see Servie on the front patio. She was pacing nervously. One hand on her hip and the other shading her face against the bright desert sun. She was clearly looking – searching. As the missionaries climbed out of their car they heard Servie yell, "Penny. Penny!"

Pork usually finds itself on Easter tables every year, but in this home, Penny the pig was a treasured pink pet. A pink pet that has no business wandering the Arizona desert. A gate was accidentally left open and she was off and running.

Servie grabbed at her heart when she saw the missionaries.

"Thank goodness you are here! I don't know what to do! Help me please! Penny is lost. It belongs to Angela," she cried.

The missionaries spread out. Divide and conquer was the

idea. One searched inside the house just in case. Another ran to the backyard. Servie kept watch out front with the third.

Servie had already called the neighbors. No answer.

"We need more help," Servie said. "Come with me and let's drive."

Homes were spread some distance in this high desert area. There were acres of harsh, thorny terrain. Certainly, there were plenty of desert animal dwellers happy to add pig to their food chain. The missionaries piled into Servie's car.

"Let's say a prayer," one of the missionaries said.

Everyone quickly responded with bowed heads and closed eyes. They were praying for a little pink pig.

A quick amen and they were off – speeding down the road. Eyes fixed on the landscape. Mustering all the faith they could. Believing that He had heard.

"Stop! I see the pig!" yelled one of the missionaries.

Servie screeched to a halt. Doors opened and three missionaries piled out of the car. Down in a desert wash they looked where the missionary was pointing. They saw a flash of pink. Penny was racing through her new-found playground. How had she seen that from the car? Incredible.

They quickly surrounded Penny, determined to grab and not let go. But this pig had other things in mind. It darted to the right, then to the left, then back onto the road up the hill toward home.

Three missionaries dressed in skirts sprinting up the street. Chasing a little pink pig. And this little pig was screaming –

"Wee … wee … wee …" All the way home.

Three missionaries came to teach Servie that day. Now they sat in her home and listened as Servie taught them. She pointed to her heart and explained the pain that she was feeling earlier.

Desperation. Fear.

"Then I saw your car," Servie whispered.

A tender mercy combined with a scheduled appointment.

Missionaries sent to help. Living what they teach. Service – prayer – unwavering faith.

"What is the date?" she asked the missionaries. "I will write this in my journal so that I will never forget this miracle."

Servie placed her hand on her heart. Prayers and a little pink pig. A nursery rhyme come to life. With a little help from Him.

. . .

Servie listened intently. The missionaries were over again with the next-door neighbors from church and they were helping Servie understand the scriptures better. Learning didn't stop with the baptism. Studying the scriptures was a lifelong process and Servie appreciated the help. Sometimes she read from her English scriptures. And sometimes she pulled out those in her native language of Zulu.

Servie's family was supportive of this decision to join a new church. They could hear the excitement in her voice when she would talk about what she had learned and the people at church who had befriended her. They were happy that she had found peace and joy.

Today the missionaries were talking and studying about prayer. A reminder that this spiritual form of communication was real. Heavenly Father was interested and always listening. The scriptures testified over and over. It was a process of asking and having faith that He would answer the righteous desires of our hearts.

Scriptures were referenced and greater understanding was gained. Servie already had a testimony of this. After all, a pig was found. Certainly, an answer to a desperate prayer. *If he can answer a prayer about a pig …*

Servie's heart began to pound.

"What if I pray for Heavenly Father to help me get Kimberly?" Servie said.

It was an honest question. One she hoped this little group could help her with.

All eyes were on Servie. All hearts beating for her.

"We can absolutely pray for that, Servie. We can ask for a specific blessing to help bring her home. Together we will pray and if it is Heavenly Father's will that it happens, then we can have faith that He will make it work."

Together they bowed their heads. They prayed for Kimberly. They prayed for the government officials. They prayed for the paperwork. A simple gathering with a weighty request. All hearts desiring and requesting that somehow this mother be reunited with her daughter.

Servie hugged her friends. With moist eyes, she thanked them for caring. Servie wanted this answer to a prayer more than anything in her life. She believed Heavenly Father heard it. Servie turned it over to Him. It was all she could do. She would find her faith and hold tight.

It was her last hope.

. . .

An invitation to pray is the single most mentioned commandment in all recorded scripture and is the most basic form of personal worship. To pray is to speak with God – not at Him, but with Him. He loves each of us perfectly. He is full of mercy and understanding. And He knows everything about us.

We can pray vocally or by forming thoughts and expressions in our minds. We learn through scripture that He knows the fervent petitions for specific needs and desires of our hearts[1] – "*I the Lord search the heart …*" (Jeremiah 17:10).

It is so difficult when sincere prayers and desires of our heart are not answered the way we want or when we want – like now! Our timing is different than His timing. We wonder why our exercise of deep and sincere faith from an obedient life does not immediately bring the desired result.

This mortal life is an experience in profound trust – trust in Jesus Christ. Trust in His teachings. Trust in our capacity to be led by the Holy Spirit. To trust means to obey willingly without knowing the end from the beginning.

"Trust in the Lord with all thine heart; and lean not unto thine own understanding.

In all thy ways acknowledge him, and he shall direct thy paths" (Proverbs 3:5-6).

To exercise faith is to trust that the Lord knows what He is doing with you. It is trusting that He can accomplish it for your eternal good even though you cannot understand or imagine how He can possibly do it. It is doing all you can, but ultimately turning your heart with all your righteous desires over to Him.

When we pass through trials for His purposes, He will help us as we trust and exercise faith in Him. Often that support will come step by step – a little portion at a time. We must position our hearts to feel that help. It is evidence of His continuing love and compassion. The Lord will place in your path packets of spiritual sunlight to brighten your way. They often come after the trial has been the greatest. If we recognize and remember, it will change our relationship with the Lord. Our love for Him and trust in Him deepens.[2]

. . .

It was just an ordinary day. Hot, dry temperatures and sunshine. A consistent standard for living in the desert. Servie had errands to run for Angela and was headed back to the house.

"*Better stop and get the mail.*" Servie pulled the car over and got out to unlock the box. She reached into the container and retrieved the pile of mail. Bills and more bills. Advertisements. And so much junk mail.

It was the return address that suddenly caught her eye. United States Immigration. Servie felt her stomach drop. Her heart began to race. She dropped everything else and tore open the envelope.

Her eyes quickly scanned the letter. Darting back and forth to understand the words.

"Ohhhhhh!"

Servie screamed. She threw her hands up in the air and jumped up and down waving the letter. Kimberly's paperwork had been approved by the government to bring her to the United States. Servie picked up the rest of the mail and ran to the car. She drove much too fast down the roads leading to her home.

"Angela! Angela!" Servie screamed as she ran inside the house. "It's a miracle!"

Angela came running at the commotion.

"What happened, Servie?" Angela replied. The look on Servie's face told her it was something good.

"Kimberly has been approved! Look!"

Servie thrust the letter into Angela's hands.

"Oh, Angela it is truly a miracle. God has heard our prayers. Just days ago, the missionaries and I prayed. We prayed for Kimberly to come here. Look what God has done!"

Angela quickly glanced over the cover letter. It was true. Kimberly's paperwork had been approved by the United States government. All that was needed now was to take that paperwork to the embassy in Zimbabwe and bring this child home.

"Oh, Servie! This is so incredible!" Angela said.

Together they grabbed onto each other and jumped up and down. Hooting and hollering. It was a mighty celebration!

Both women embraced and cried. What an unbelievable journey. They looked again and again at the letter. Almost not believing what they saw in black and white.

"We must tell everybody!" Servie said.

They both picked up their phones and starting making phone calls and placing announcements on social media. They wanted everybody to know about this miracle.

Servie paused and suddenly remembered.

"Oh, I must call the missionaries right away!" Servie said. "They will be so happy to hear the good news!"

She considered their part in this. They truly had changed Servie's life.

. . .

Servie stood back to survey her piles. Once again, she was bringing more than could possibly fit into one suitcase. A few things for herself and plenty of clothing for the orphans. She would pay for the second suitcase. It was worth every penny. She thought of the smiles on the children's faces from her last visit.

What joy she felt in her heart. Every trip to Zimbabwe over the years she had dreamed of this opportunity. Finally, she would be returning to the United States with Kimberly. She patted her heart and acknowledged the gratitude she felt for God granting this miracle. Tomorrow could not come soon enough.

Servie heard a light tap on the door. She turned to see Angela smiling.

"I see you're busy getting packed, Servie. I have a surprise," said Angela. Her eyes were shining with anticipation.

Servie put her hands on her hips and smiled.

"What surprise? What are you talking about?"

"I found a ticket to Zimbabwe. I'm going with you to pick up Kimberly!" Angela said.

Servie threw her hands up in the air then ran over to wrap her arms around this dearest friend.

"Oh, there could be nothing better! This will be beautiful! There are so many people for you to meet. My mom. My brother and his wife. All my friends and neighbors who have heard so much about you!" cried Servie. "And Kimberly …"

Servie felt a lump of emotion in her throat as she thought about that. Her daughter was one of so many connections between these two friends. Now she and Angela would share in this new celebrated reunion.

"And you will meet my Kimberly. You know so much about her, but have never really met her in person. Oh, Angela how wonderful! Thank you so much. How will I ever sleep tonight? I am so happy."

Angela smiled. It had taken some effort to rearrange her schedule to make this last-minute trip. But something told her that she needed to make it happen. She had heard a voice. A week ago, she woke one morning with an overwhelming feeling that she had to go to Africa – immediately – not in two years as the family had planned. The feeling was so strong she had called her husband very early in the morning. He was traveling for work.

"I woke up with this almost suffocating feeling that if we don't go with Servie now to get Kimberly, she's never going to get her out of Africa. She'll never leave Zimbabwe," Angela explained.

He listened and heard the conviction and urgency in her voice. He knew that she knew this was important. She was following an impression. Those impressions in her life had never steered her in the wrong direction. He trusted her.

"I can't leave my work right now," replied her husband. "But you go."

"You want me to go to Zimbabwe without you?" The thought was a bit overwhelming.

"You can do this," he said. His confidence and support was clear. "Just make sure you bring Kimberly home."

. . .

Word spread quickly. Servie was coming home to Zimbabwe for her annual visit and bringing her friend Angela. Servie's family and friends knew this was a special relationship. They had heard so many stories. They knew Angela had been so kind to her. Everyone was eager to finally meet this friend.

"You know, sometimes there are angels right here on earth," Servie had told her family. "Angela is my angel."

Many had gathered at the home of Servie's brother. When the two women walked in the door, it set off a joyous celebration. Hugs were exchanged by all. Even the food was festive! Beautiful colors of fruits and vegetables from gardens in the village. It was a sight to see. Angela took every opportunity to speak with each member of this dear family that she had learned to love through Servie's stories.

Servie found Kimberly in the maze of celebration. She was home on holiday from the boarding school. Servie ran over and wrapped her arms around her.

"Oh, my Kimberly. How I've missed you!" cried Servie.

"I've missed you, too … Mom," replied Kimberly.

Since Kimberly had learned that Auntie Servie was really her mom, she wanted to call her by that name. She still had the mom who raised her in Zimbabwe. That would never change. But she had decided that it was wonderful to have two moms. She knew both moms loved her more than anything.

Servie's heart swelled. To hear Kimberly refer to her again as "mom" was indescribable. She stifled a sob in her throat. What a long journey this had been. She could see the end. A multitude of emotions swirled within her soul.

"I have something to tell you, Kimberly," Servie said. "I brought papers. Papers that give me permission to bring you over to the United States. You could finish high school there. Instead of going back to your school in two weeks, we could fly together back to my home in Arizona. What do you think about that? Would you like to go with me?"

Kimberly's eyes widened. This was a new development. Servie recognized it as a huge change for this child. Surely there would be conflicting emotions. Leaving her family and friends in Zimbabwe to make a new life across the world.

Kimberly smiled. The United States. Better schools and a better life. This is what she and her friends talked about when exchanging views on their dreams. It was a competition of sorts to see who would go where. Friends had gone to France, the Philippines, New Zealand and Australia. They worked hard at school to qualify for scholarships in other parts of the world. She had seen older girls with high grade marks on school records leave Zimbabwe for fun and exciting opportunities. They all knew it was the ticket out of the country. An exit door which would determine their future. This was happening a bit earlier than she had thought. But it felt right.

"I'd like that. Yes, Mom, I want to go with you."

Kimberly clung tight to her mother. This adventure would be a bit frightening. But Kimberly had always had a deep connection to this woman who for so many years was Auntie Servie. She felt safe with her. Loved by her.

Later that week Servie took Angela out to the country to meet her mom. The neighbors had all gathered together and family and friends sat out on the front porch and told stories from the past. Servie's mother couldn't speak English, but she understood some. Servie and Kimberly helped with the translation so that Angela didn't miss a single detail.

Servie's mother laughed as her daughter and Angela carried on about their lives in the United States. She watched them closely. Remembering a time years ago when blacks and whites didn't carry on together. Apartheid. It was a different time. A frightening time. Of all her children, Servie had never seen color. She was quick to forgive and never to judge. A walking definition of peace and love. They could all learn from this friendship. The conversation paused.

She pointed to Angela and then to Servie and spoke.

Servie laughed and then translated for Angela.

"My mother says she has twins. One came out white and one came out black," Servie said.

Everybody laughed. What a wonder to all be together. A perfect day. It was a treasured moment.

Servie stood up. "We have something for you, Angela. She wants to show you. It's a gift from our family. In this country, we give a gift to honor a special visitor. We all decided this should be your gift."

Angela was touched by the surprise announcement. This was not expected.

"Come, follow me," Servie said. "We want to show you."

They walked over to a small pasture of grass. There were milk cows grazing in the field. Servie walked up to one of the cows.

"This is your cow, Angela. It provides milk. There is a boy in this village who is taking care of the cow. We pay him to take care of it here. But it is yours."

Angela turned and looked into the eyes of this loving family. What a beautiful tribute. She would never forget this. She felt a deep reverence for the sacrifice and token that this represented. She understood it had deep meaning. She would name the cow. *Joy* seemed appropriate.

"And that goat over there. It is yours as well. A gift from my mother," said Servie.

"Thank you so much," Angela said.

Angela looked back at Servie's mother – the matriarch of this entire family. What a beautiful woman. She had sacrificed, worked hard and loved for so many years. Servie's mother had never been schooled, but learned to speak the Zulu language in her village.

When her husband died early in their marriage, she had been left alone to support and care for all her children. And she did that in part through her little gathering of livestock. Angela met the gaze of this great woman and nodded.

"This goat I will name Hope," Angela said.

Servie's mother responded with a slow nod and glistening eyes. Their eyes locked. Language was not necessary. It was understood.

. . .

Once again, the villagers gathered together in a festive spirit. Fresh, beautiful food. Colorful decorations. It was a goodbye celebration for Kimberly. Members of the village church choir and neighbors had come to support this family in sending this daughter off. They brought presents and thoughtful keepsakes for Kimberly.

There were mixed emotions in this group. They loved Servie and rejoiced in the idea that her daughter would now join her in the United States. It was a miracle from God and they knew it. But they had loved Kimberly for all of her life here. This was going to be hard to watch her leave.

Plans were announced that Servie and Angela would go to the embassy the following day and get the necessary paperwork finished for Kimberly's departure. Hugs and cheers were exchanged by all. Finally, an end to a story filled with tragedy and years of separation. Tomorrow could not come soon enough.

. . .

It was the day before Servie and Angela were scheduled to leave Zimbabwe. They both woke up early in the morning to head out with the paperwork. Their destination was the embassy in Harare. It was a 6-hour drive from the village. Servie's brother had taken work off to be their driver. He knew what they were up against in road blocks. Kimberly would stay back with family and begin packing things up. They would return with her visa and gather together for one final dinner.

Six times they were stopped on the way to Harare. It was unnerving. Angela had never experienced this kind of intimidation.

"Why are they doing this?" Angela asked.

"Well, they are hoping to find something wrong so they can bribe us," Servie replied.

Angela just couldn't believe it. She had already paid a huge bribe to bring two suitcases of medical supplies and school supplies past the customs agent. This was a new world.

Finally, they arrived at the embassy. The office was hot and humid. Both women took a position in line and waited for their turn at the desk. There were very limited and specific timeframes to handle this kind of immigration paperwork. Only one hour of time on Tuesdays and Thursdays. Hopefully this was a quick task of pulling Kimberly's paperwork and receiving her visa.

Finally, it was their turn. Servie placed the papers received from the United States government on the desk and made the request for Kimberly's visa. The officer looked at the paperwork and then at Servie. She repositioned her glasses on her nose and clicked some keys on the computer. After several minutes, she pushed the papers back at Servie.

"I'm afraid that will be impossible," she said. "We have no record of your daughter's papers. We need legal paperwork to prove that you are her mother and that you are requesting her to leave this country."

"That's impossible!" Servie cried. "My lawyer back in Indiana assured me that he had filed the paperwork. He told me that we just needed clearance from the United States and I have that now." Servie started falling apart.

The officer looked back at the computer.

"There is no record of paperwork. How do we even know that you are Kimberly's mother? Show me a picture of your daughter," she said coarsely.

"I – I don't have one," Servie replied. I don't have a phone that has pictures. You see I left her when she was just a baby and I come here every year to see her."

Servie felt sick. Her heart was racing so fast she thought she might pass out.

"Let me see your signature on a receipt for a doctor's visit. A childcare receipt. Anything that would prove you are her mother," she blurted out.

Servie knew she couldn't produce those things. It would be her sister-in-law's signature on those documents because she had been responsible for raising Kimberly. The situation had quickly gone from bad to worse. The tension in Servie's chest was heightened along with the sense of foreboding that this would never work. What this must look like to the officer. She felt embarrassment. Humiliation. She dropped her head in defeat and started bawling. Angela stepped in.

"Servie, go over and sit down. Let me figure out what's going on," Angela whispered.

All Angela's senses were firing. There must be answers. She was determined to figure this out. She leaned over the desk and looked directly at the officer.

"Of course, she's her mother! Please, look again ma'am," she said. "There must be a mistake. This woman has paid her attorney thousands of dollars to produce the paperwork needed. He assured her it was taken care of."

"The paperwork has not been filed. The visa is denied," the officer said.

Angela paused. She chose her words carefully.

"We have traveled a far distance to bring this woman's daughter home to the United States. Please help me understand. I would like to help my friend," Angela said.

The officer looked up at Angela's pleading eyes. Then glanced over at the sobbing woman in the chair. Perhaps this was worth another look. The officer turned back toward her computer and began to search. Researching anything that might link them to an answer. Finally, after several minutes she shook her head and looked up at Angela.

"Angela, if I had to bet, I'd say those papers are probably still on some lawyer's desk," she reported.

"That's not the story we heard from the lawyer in Indiana," Angela replied. Angela wondered if this officer was just making up excuses or whether she was being honest with her.

"I will email him today and we will be back. Can you please write down exactly what is required? The form numbers … anything."

The officer wrote down what was needed. She then looked up at Angela.

"We're dealing with a minor here. When it involves a minor, we expedite it. It goes to the front of the line," explained the officer.

"Thank you for your help," Angela replied. She forced a smile, grateful for the help extended by this woman.

Angela walked over to where Servie was sitting. Still in a puddle of tears. She grabbed her hands and pulled her to her feet. Together they walked out the door.

"Servie, we need to find an internet café. I need to email your attorney – now."

. . .

Angela paid the fee for a block of time on the internet. She sat down and located the email address of Servie's attorney back in Indiana. Quickly she pulled out her phone and began to type the message – *I'm rather confused. I am in Zimbabwe to bring a child home and the embassy has no record of her – ever …*

The attorney swiftly responded – *First of all I never told Servie that the papers were ready …* Immediately Angela doubted this man's integrity. Servie would not make up something like that. The attorney continued – *The truth is when we moved our offices, I lost Servie's file for six months. You need to hire somebody to go search through all my records in storage …*

Angela couldn't believe it. After fuming for several minutes, she took a deep breath and wrote back – *You know I understand how sometimes these things can happen, but let me tell you what's going to happen next. You will fill out and file the following form numbers and you will pay the expedited fee at your expense. If there are any additional fees to be paid to the United States government you will be paying them. And this will be done by 5:00 p.m. tomorrow.*

The attorney replied – *Well, I'm not sure that is possible.*

Now Angela was unhappy. Her fingers typed her reply and

conveyed her resolve. *Let me remind you again. You **will** fill out the papers. I'm not asking. You will do it. And you will file them or I will be calling the Attorney General in the state of Indiana …*

. . .

"I can't leave you here," Servie cried. "It is not safe for you to be here in Harare by yourself. Promise me you won't come back here."

Servie was terrified. How would Angela survive Harare? A white woman alone in a very different culture and very dangerous city.

Angela looked at her dear friend who had tears in her eyes.

"I can't promise that, Servie. I cannot make that promise. I told you I was coming here to bring this child home and I'm bringing her home," Angela said. As soon as the words were out, Angela hoped that she could do just that.

Angela had received an email from the embassy two days after the emailed conversation with the attorney in Indiana. The paperwork had been filed and they included a long list of needed items. Physicals, chest X-rays, vaccinations, background checks, passport photos. It was overwhelming, but moving in the right direction. Angela was determined to stay and see this through.

"Please," whispered Servie. It's not safe."

Servie's visa had expired and she had to return or risk all kinds of trouble. She had never predicted that Kimberly wouldn't be on that plane with her. The whole circus of events in the last 24 hours was unthinkable.

"Go," Angela said. "I will be okay. You know I'm a big girl. I can handle this." Angela had talked to her husband and told him what was going on. His advice to her was that she was absolutely right. His advice – stay and get it done.

Angela took Servie into her arms then stepped back and grasped her hands in hers.

"I'm not leaving here without Kimberly," she said. "Go. I'll email you every day and let you know what's happening."

Once again Servie turned and willed her legs to carry her onto the airplane. So many times, she had cried and cried on trips home. This was different. She was terrified for her friend. But Angela had insisted. Servie's heart was heavy. The fear was overtaking the faith. This would be a long, long trip home.

. . .

Angela placed her phone down on the desk. She cradled her head in her hands. This was becoming increasingly difficult. Angela had secured a hotel in Harare for herself and Kimberly so that they could attend to all the requirements listed by the embassy. Finally, she had reached the one doctor authorized by the embassy to give Kimberly a physical exam. Angela had hired a driver for the day. On one side of town was the chest X-ray. Then they had to pick up the vaccine at a pharmacy and drive across the city to deliver it to the doctor so Kimberly could receive it. Passport pictures. Other documents filled out and signed. Fees required for this and for that. They raced through the city.

The driver pulled up in front of the Federal Police Department. Kimberly would need a background check. Angela was tired from the heat and the demands of the day. Kimberly was exhausted as well, but she knew Angela was working hard to get things done. Kimberly would do whatever Angela asked. Kimberly liked her – trusted her.

Angela noted the barbed wire fencing surrounding this building. It was intimidating. She told the driver to wait as she and Kimberly got out of the back seat. Together they walked through the front doors. The police officer at the front desk listened as Angela requested to see somebody about a background check for Kimberly. She explained that the embassy was waiting for it.

"That will take 30 days," the police officer stated. There was no emotion in his voice. He wiped a bead of sweat from his forehead.

"We don't have 30 days," Angela replied. "Is there an expedited way to get this done? What's the fee to get it expedited?" Angela tried to remain calm, but confident.

"For $50 more you can get it done in three days," he answered.

"I really need these papers today," Angela replied. Now she had his attention. He raised one eyebrow.

"Follow me. Let's go to my office," he stated.

Angela noticed the security guards and the barbed wire fencing and bars on the windows once again as she and Kimberly followed the officer back into a room.

"Have a seat," the officer said. He motioned toward two chairs and then turned and left.

Angela considered whether this really was a good idea. She was arguing and pushing this man because she wanted to mark another item off the impossibly long list of requirements. But she hoped this wasn't a mistake. Minutes later the officer returned and sat across the desk and looked at Kimberly. He asked her a few general background questions. She answered them. Then the officer looked directly at Angela.

"Be back here at 2:00 and you can bring me something to drink," he demanded. Angela was used to taking people literally. It was hot. Surely, he would like a nice cold soda.

"You want a 7Up or a coke?"

He stared at her. No answer. Then the realization hit Angela – *that* kind of drink. She was so out of her element. How naïve. She was not used to all this bribing.

"Okay, no problem," she added. "See you at 2:00."

Fortunately, the driver was still out front. She had paid him for the entire day. But even that was no guarantee. They drove to a local store, purchased the drink and headed back to the Federal Police Department. Angela placed the money and the liquid bribe on the desk. In exchange, the officer handed the paperwork to Angela. Transaction complete.

The driver raced through the city streets to the Embassy. She told the driver they were on an important deadline. All items on the checklist had been satisfied. Angela was anxious to make it there before closing. The hours were so restrictive. She didn't want to wait until next week for another immigration time slot.

Angela and Kimberly walked into the embassy with two minutes to spare. Once again, they had to get through the security checkpoint and then find an officer to see them. She had everything neatly organized in one large file. Surely, this would satisfy them. She pushed the file in front of the officer. This woman was no stranger in this office. She had been a relentless visitor. Constantly checking on things and asking questions. He looked through the items. Mentally checking off forms and other requirements.

"We'll be in touch," he growled.

"*Really? We'll be in touch?*" Angela thought. Very anticlimactic after days of racing through traffic and meeting deadlines. *We'll be in touch?* Angela shook her head as she left the embassy. A disappointing response. She had hoped to return to the hotel with more encouragement than that.

. . .

Angela woke up to sunlight filtering through the window. Another day of heat. Another day of humidity. Another day spent in this Harare hotel. It had been four weeks since Servie left Zimbabwe. Weeks of jumping through hoops to gather documents. Fees required for everything.

In the time spent gathering documents and driving, Angela had seen things in Harare that broke her heart: children who should be in school were instead standing in the middle of a four-lane street with a baby tied to their backs begging for money; boys sleeping on the ground because that was their home; no families; boys thrown out on the street because they were products of rape or their parents had died of AIDS.

They were street boys. They stayed together, slept under shade trees and ate what they could find. The poorest person in the United States had more than most in Zimbabwe. It made her shudder.

Danger throughout the city was evident. The hotel staff didn't allow their customers to leave the premises without an escort. They would send a guard with Angela just to purchase a book at the bookstore across the street. Because of the unsafe conditions, all meals were eaten at the hotel. It was certainly a lesson in both awareness and humility.

Angela reached for her phone to check her email. She

wondered what the day would bring. It was a twisted tale of demands and waiting. More demands. Then more waiting. Angela wasn't sure which was worse – meeting the demands or waiting for the next one. It was a vicious cycle buried in government bureaucracy and red tape.

Her phone showed new communication from the embassy. They wanted more proof that Servie was Kimberly's biological mother. Last week they had demanded more pictures. Angela had emailed Servie and had her notify everyone in the family. They gathered any pictures they had of Servie and Kimberly together. Pictures from every trip to Zimbabwe that Servie had done over the years. Hadn't that been enough? Now they wanted more.

A document was required from the hospital where Kimberly was born. They wanted an affidavit that Servie was a patient on a specific date and that she had given birth to a female child. That date was Kimberly's birth date. Another hoop. Another item added to the list.

Angela emailed Servie to tell her of the request. It was one more brick in the impossible wall before them. Angela felt like she held a chisel and was trying to break down the wall one nugget at a time. Would it ever be enough?

Servie emailed back immediately. She was so discouraged. She just wanted her friend to get on an airplane and come back home. She didn't trust the Zimbabwe government to ever release her daughter. It had been too much.

Angela's own daughter had asked her if she was ever coming home. Two weeks away had turned into so much more. But Angela's husband stood firm in his support. *Don't lose faith. If anyone can get this done – you can.* He was a constant ally and continued to rally her cause.

Angela thought back to the quiet voice that had prompted this visit. It was all she had left. The rational thing to do would be to give up and just go home. She had tried. She had really tried. She had never worked so hard in her life.

But that voice. Angela's ability to hear and follow that voice had been a gift since she was a little girl. It had saved her from harm. It had led her to paths she would never have discovered. She had learned over her lifetime to trust that voice. Angela wasn't in Zimbabwe for herself. She wasn't fighting battles for Servie. She was there because God wanted Kimberly out of that country. God needed someone on that ground. And that someone was Angela. She knew she was on His errand.

Hot, desperate tears rolled down her cheeks as she considered her position of fighting against this government in a foreign country. She must continue to do this. More tears flowed. Maddened tears of resolve to fight and win this battle. She silently prayed that God would replace her fear with strength.

Angela felt a small hand on her back.

"It's okay, Mama Angela. I will be fine here. If it doesn't work out, I'll be fine."

It was Kimberly. At fifteen, she was mature enough to recognize the reality of the situation. She gently patted this kind woman on the back. She trusted this woman. Felt a kinship and love already. She had decided weeks earlier to call her Mama Angela. Kimberly had felt an immediate connection to her the first day they met. She could see the toll this was taking on her. Tears of anguish told the story.

Angela turned to face Kimberly. She paused for a moment to gather her emotion and looked into this beautiful girl's eyes.

"Kimberly – I'm not leaving this country without you. We are going to America together."

As soon as the words came out of Angela's mouth she knew that only God could deliver this promise. She had crossed every bridge that she knew how to cross and was still fighting the battle. The promise to Kimberly had just fallen out of her mouth. She hoped that God had inspired the promise.

Once again Angela dug deep and found strength. She would meet the demands of this foreign government and walk into the embassy with papers in hand. Hopefully her continued return visits would send a message. Today she must partner with God and take another step.

Angela found a quiet moment and reverently bowed her head in gratitude. She acknowledged God's hand in her life and asked for his continued inspiration and direction this day. She expressed gratitude for God's divine guidance that she had witnessed on more than one occasion in the last four weeks.

Kimberly bowed her own head and joined in prayer. She prayed for Mama Angela. She prayed for her two moms. One in Zimbabwe and another waiting for her in the United States. With all the faith she possessed in her young heart, Kimberly prayed for a miracle.

. . .

The officer looked across the desk at Angela. He shook his head. This woman would not give up. Over and over again she continued to come back with more documents. Today was no different. She had returned with the newest request. He placed the documents on the desk and leafed through the various pages.

He took his pen and initialed several of the documents. Then pulled a stamp out of the drawer and banged it across several of the papers. He quickly gathered them together and slammed a stapler down on the corner. His fingers clicked along the keyboard as new updates were entered into his computer. Then he reached into a drawer, pulled out a piece of paper and placed it directly in front of Angela. There was an inch-thick packet on the corner of his desk. He reached over and slid the packet across the desk so that it lay between them.

"Sign the paper," he ordered. "This is an affidavit swearing that you will not let this packet out of sight until you turn it over to immigration at the port of entry. If it is opened in any fashion it will become null and void."

Angela had no idea what was in the sealed packet. But she knew it contained freedom. The officer rolled a pen across the desk. She picked up the pen and signed the sworn statement. Then Angela looked up at the officer for further direction.

He met Angela's eyes. Her blue eyes wide in anticipation of his response.

"Visa for Kimberly is approved," he said.

Angela stared at the officer. Suddenly the realization hit. A myriad of emotions surged throughout Angela's body. Her mind raced through five agonizing weeks of detail. She blinked hard then slowly nodded her head at the officer.

"Thank you," she said.

Then Angela picked up the packet and turned and quietly walked toward the front doors. She would likely never enter this office again. Her legs wanted to collapse, but she steadied herself and continued forward, pushing the door open.

She looked for the paid driver. He was still waiting. She needed an internet connection.

"Take me back to the hotel please," she asked.

Once inside Angela reached down inside her purse and found her phone. She pulled it out and tried to focus on the screen. She scrolled down and found Servie's email address.

Angela's fingers trembled as she attempted to write the message. Angela felt her heart swell with gratitude. Recognizing that a miracle had just taken place. She recognized the whisperings of the Spirit. Her heart pounded. Tears filled her eyes. She quickly read the message then hit the send button.

Kimberly's visa is approved. We are coming home!

CHAPTER 9

A Song of Hope

*"Love recognizes no barriers. It jumps hurdles,
leaps fences, penetrates walls to arrive at its
destination full of hope."*

Maya Angelou

Servie picked up the phone and called the missionaries.

"Kimberly's coming home!" Servie screamed. "She got the visa. Angela's bringing her home tomorrow. I'm meeting them at the airport at 9:00 a.m."

The missionaries cheered. They had been fasting and praying with Servie for weeks. What a beautiful miracle indeed. It was an incredible example to these two young women of God's love for his children. An example of answered prayers. An experience that both would never forget.

"We'll call everyone and spread the good news," said the missionaries.

. . .

Late that night Servie reached over and turned on the lamp next to her bed. She pulled her bible from the nightstand onto her lap. Tomorrow's prospect was preventing her from sleeping.

She had learned to appreciate what God wanted her to know from reading the scriptures. She opened the book and the pages opened to Matthew.

"But seek ye first the kingdom of God, and his righteousness; and all these things shall be added unto you" (Matthew 6:33).

Servie considered the promise. *All these things shall be added.* The gospel had brought so many gifts into her life. An eternal perspective, peace, love, and a miracle. So many stories in the bible testified of miracles. Servie knew that miracles are still happening. Tomorrow was proof of that.

Servie tossed and turned for most of the night. Eventually she rolled over and looked at the time on the clock next to her bed. It was early dawn. Well before the sun was up. Servie had hardly slept. A few minutes' doze here and there just to be woken up by the sound of her heart beating. Servie's emotions were raw and heightened. This day had finally arrived.

There had been a stream of texts from Angela giving constant updates.

We are boarding the plane in Zimbabwe.
We are in South Africa now.
We are finally boarding to America.
We are in the Atlanta airport.

Servie knew that Kimberly and Angela were in the air somewhere between Atlanta, Georgia, and Phoenix, Arizona. She jumped up to get ready. She couldn't lay in bed and wait. She would drive very early to the airport in downtown Phoenix and wait there.

. . .

Servie found the flight monitors and carefully looked down

the list to find the flight from Atlanta. The plane was on time and Servie was very early. That was okay. This is where she needed to be. Servie checked the gate number and walked down the corridor to an area where passengers would emerge after landing. After several minutes, she located the area and quietly took a seat.

There was a buzz of passenger noise and conversation in the area. Hurried passengers heading through security and tired passengers coming up the walkway from recent flight arrivals. Families laughing. Families crying. Wide spectrums of emotion on display. So many visuals. So many stories.

"If they only knew mine," Servie thought.

Soon the scene of the airport seemed to just disappear. Sounds were muted. Servie's thoughts found her own story unfolding before her. The death of her father. The birth of five beautiful children with her husband. And then his death and the birth of little number six. She remembered the heartache of leaving those children to provide for them. She would do anything for them. Then death again. Even today on this joyous occasion she missed her sons. And sweet Sithabile. The heartbreak and the desperation had been almost too much. How she had tried so hard to bring Kimberly here. Too many years. Fifteen years of childhood she could never bring back.

But today was a new beginning. Years of memories which culminated in this moment. Servie felt a wave of emotions so strong that she could barely contain it. Powerful feelings from the past combined with the joy of today. A pure and all-embracing joy.

Servie felt her eyes fill with tears. Raw, emotional sensations consumed her senses. Servie wanted to weep.

Not here. Not now.

Servie took a long, deep breath, as if to warn the threatening breakdown. She would allow the tears later tonight. She wanted to greet Kimberly and Angela with happiness and elation. As she had done so many times, Servie wanted to be strong.

Servie stood and paced the floor. It should be any moment now. She kept her eyes on the passengers.

All at once they appeared. Servie could see both Kimberly and Angela making their way up the long corridor. She jumped in celebration and ran up to get a closer look. Their happy, tired faces explained it all.

"Oh – you're here! You're here!" Servie cried.

Servie grabbed her daughter and pulled her in close. This was no dream – it was real. They clung tight, both understanding the significance.

Servie looked over to her friend's weary face. She wrapped her arms around Angela's neck and buried her head into her shoulder. What this friend had done for her – how could she ever find the words to thank her?

Three women stood together. Hands clasped. Faces beaming. Recognizing the significance.

"Let's go home," Servie whispered.

. . .

In the hour-long drive home from the airport, Angela filled Servie in on all the latest developments. The difficulties in Zimbabwe. The lists of requirements. The miracles that opened so many doors. It was an incredible ordeal. No one had predicted so many roadblocks.

The car pulled up the steep driveway and made the turn over to the front of the house. Servie gasped. Every door and surface had been decorated for Kimberly. There were ribbons and posters honoring the arrival of Kimberly. After Servie left for the airport earlier that morning, the missionaries and friends from church had come and put it all up.

"This is for me?" Kimberly said. She was in awe of the attention. She felt so welcome. It was a wonderful tribute.

Servie and Angela took it all in. What beautiful friends they had here. The church had changed both of their lives. Loving, generous people who had become like family. Servie put her arm around Kimberly and gave her a playful squeeze. They stepped back and looked at the display. Kind, welcoming words of love displayed everywhere.

Servie escorted the weary travelers into the home. These two needed some sleep. They had been up for days of travel. Angela and Kimberly needed a hot shower and a bed.

As they entered the front door of the home, Servie felt the wall of emotion that she had suppressed at the airport. It was trying to break through. She looked back at Kimberly. She was here. There was something about crossing the threshold with her. This was real. Kimberly was home.

Kimberly saw the emotion.

"Are you okay, Mom?" she said.

"These are happy tears," Servie replied. "This is a beautiful day."

Kimberly agreed. She felt loved … by three moms. Her mom in Zimbabwe, her mom in Arizona and Mama Angela. This new life was so different from her village back in Zimbabwe. Just the car ride from the airport home had been filled with new sights and sounds from the big city. But it felt right. She wanted to see everything. Embrace her new surroundings. But first she needed to sleep for a bit. Servie escorted her daughter into her new bedroom. They would unpack later.

Servie closed her daughter's bedroom door. She walked down the hallway to her own bedroom. She entered and sat in the chair by the window. Not sure her legs could hold her up another second. She touched her chest and took a deep breath.

It was time. Servie would allow herself to feel. The wall needed to come down. She opened up the gates and let the tears fall. She talked to her Heavenly Father. Shared with Him her feelings. She knew He understood.

Then Servie buried her face in her hands and wept.

. . .

The church organ came to life and music spilled into the chapel from the large pipes on the wall. Servie felt her spirit soar. It was her favorite hymn. The words were permanently etched on her heart. A beautiful hymn which perfectly described her love and gratitude for the Lord. Servie closed her eyes and felt the words as the congregation sang the last verse.

He lives! All glory to his name!
He lives, my Savior, still the same.
Oh, sweet the joy this sentence gives:
"I know that my Redeemer lives!"[1]

Kimberly had thrown herself into her new surroundings. She attended church with her mother and Angela. The congregation welcomed her with open arms and the other teenagers and youth leaders made her feel loved and included. She had asked to learn more about this new church and so missionaries taught her the gospel. She learned about eternal families – what a glorious concept! She would see her brothers again, and the father that she had never met.

Kimberly was baptized months later with new friends in attendance. Her mother and Angela were there to love and support. Kimberly could feel the peace and happiness that the gospel had brought to these two women and she wanted the same for herself. She embraced the teachings and found a new, closer relationship with God. And so once again there was a baptism overflowing with support from this new church family. An inspiring measure of unity that touched the hearts of many.

School was challenging but Kimberly focused on succeeding. She would finish her high school education in two years. Goals were set for high grades and college attendance. Kimberly had been raised to work hard. She would continue to do that here in her new environment.

Servie took a deep breath and looked toward the front. Her daughter would be addressing the congregation for the first time today. Servie was so proud of her. And Servie was nervous enough for both of them! Kimberly approached the pulpit. All eyes were on this young woman. Ears intent on what she might share this Sunday morning.

Kimberly stood up tall and spoke into the microphone with the poise and countenance of a life-long member of the church. She bore a strong testimony of the difference it was making in her life. She testified of God's love in watching over her family – here, in Zimbabwe, and in heaven. Kimberly expressed gratitude for the blessings of the gospel in her life.

"One day I want to be a missionary," she said. "I want to share what I have now learned."

. . .

There was an excitement in the air. Families gathered together for this monumental event. The room was buzzing with quietly voiced celebration.

Suddenly an announcement was made. The audience went silent.

"All rise," stated the clerk.

The judge of the United States District Court in downtown Phoenix, Arizona, entered the assembly hall. Servie and Angela and a number of friends from church stood up from their seats with all the others in attendance. The judge made his way to the podium on the stage at the front of the hall. The flag of the United States of America was in full display at the front of the room. Everyone stood with hands over hearts and recited the Pledge of Allegiance. Memorized words which took on a greater significance in this setting. There was passion and intensity.

"Thank you," the judge said. "You may be seated."

Servie turned her head. She located Kimberly sitting amongst all those who were there to receive their U.S. citizenship. It had been nine months to the day since Kimberly's feet had hit American soil. Angela had bought Kimberly a beautiful red dress for this day of celebration. The dress was both stunning and patriotic. Servie's heart swelled.

Servie looked over at Angela. What this friend had done for her. Even the day after arriving back home in the United States, Angela had made dozens of phone calls trying to secure first a new U.S. passport and then Kimberly's citizenship. It had been a huge effort to wage through more paperwork and more requirements from the United States government. It was an effort not unnoticed by Servie.

Angela turned to look at sweet Kimberly. She loved this girl. Together they had done the impossible. She had reminded Kimberly what a wonderful blessing God had given her. That when much is given – much is expected. Kimberly now had an opportunity to do great things and in nine months she had already taken that to heart. Kimberly had flourished beyond Angela's expectations. She had excelled in her new school and had made new friends. There were future dreams of college and a career in medicine. It had been incredible to witness.

The judge smiled at the crowd of hopefuls before him. He had much to say to this diverse group of individuals who were minutes away from becoming citizens of the United States.

"Your family has dreamed the dream. They have come from all parts of the world. In this country, freedom defines us. We celebrate diversity, which makes this country great."

This was a group united by opportunity and liberty. This group believed that no dream is impossible. There were many colors of skin. Multiple backgrounds and cultures all united here for the same purpose. Surely different in their journeys, but they all shared determination. You could see it in their eyes.

One by one their names were called. They had all come so far. Some by air, others by train or boat. Crossed oceans and rivers and borders to capture this dream. They were recognized for efforts that it took to get here. Now they were being asked to do just one more thing. One final task. To walk across the stage and receive their certificate of citizenship.

Servie heard Kimberly's name called. She watched as her

daughter took the walk across the stage. What a long walk it had been.

America. America. God shed His grace on thee …

Once upon a time Servie had dreams for her children. Chapters had taken her in so many directions. But this was not the end. This was the beginning. The anthem spoke to her heart.

Servie pondered her journey; recognizing where she'd been and grateful for where she was now. Years of sacrifice. Years of love.

Servie looked at her daughter and smiled. She heard the music. A song of freedom. A song of gratitude. A song of hope.

Servie's song.

CHAPTER 10

Your Song

"In the end it's not the years in your life that count. It's the life in your years."

Adlai E. Stevenson

Once upon a time …

A simple phrase that stirs our imagination. Adventure, love, mystery – all wrapped up nicely in a package entitled *happily ever after*. It is a production of storylines, music and colorful characters.

What does your melody sound like? What is your story? It is different for each one of us. The true fairy tale is learning to do God's will. Despite what is put in front of us it is once again looking for Him. Again, and again.

It is searching for the eternal happily ever after. The more we learn to do His will, the more like Him we will become. The more we become like Him, the more we will desire to live with Him in a place of beauty and peace and light beyond all conception. A place our soul longs for. A place our spirit calls home.

What is your song? Where is your fairy tale? Actually – you are living it. It is the chapters of your own book that bring you closer to God. Closer to turning your life over to Him. Trusting Him.

The chapters in your book are different than mine. Different than Servie's. The details and the characters are unique to you. But we are not alone. We all share the struggle.

There are guideposts along the way. There are patterns to follow. Principles to embrace and live. Patterns and principles which close the gap between our will and His. One chapter of our life at a time. That is the fairy tale we signed up for. The fairy tale that really does end happily ever after.

Think back to your favorite fairy tales. The main character may be a princess or a peasant. She might be a mermaid or a milkmaid. A ruler or a servant. But there is always one thing in common – sandwiched between their "once upon a time" and "happily ever after" they must all overcome adversity.

The scriptures tell us there must be opposition in all things:

"And to bring about his eternal purposes in the end of man, after he had created our first parents, and the beasts of the field and the fowls of the air, and in fine, all things which are created, it must needs be that there was an opposition; even the forbidden fruit in opposition to the tree of life; the one being sweet and the other bitter" (2 Nephi 2:15).

In stories, as in life, adversity helps to develop a depth of character and teaches us things we cannot learn otherwise.[1] We yearn for the Disney fairy tale when our perfectly laid plans crumble. A time when dreams are shattered. Life is a mess. And nothing seems fair.

Lucifer whispers that life is not fair. That if the gospel of Jesus Christ were true, we would never have problems or disappointments. But the gospel is not a guarantee against tribulation. That was Lucifer's plan. A test with no questions. The gospel of Jesus Christ is a guide for maneuvering through the challenges of life with a sense of purpose and direction.[2]

Understand that these fiery trials are designed to make

you stronger, but they have the potential to diminish or even destroy your trust in Him. They can weaken your resolve to keep your promises to Him. They take root in our weaknesses, our vulnerabilities, our sensitivities, or in the very things that matter most to us.

So how do we remain steadfast and immovable during a trial of faith? You immerse yourself in the very things that helped build your core of faith. You exercise faith in Christ. You pray and ponder the scriptures. You keep the commandments and repent, and you serve others. Whatever you do – don't step away from the church.[3]

In the New Testament, we read:

"That the trial of your faith, being much more precious than of gold that perisheth, though it be tried with fire, might be found unto praise and honour and glory at the appearing of Jesus Christ" (1 Peter 1:7).

James E. Faust said, *"Into every life there comes the painful, despairing days of adversity and buffeting. There seems to be a full measure of anguish, sorrow, and often heartbreak for everyone, including those who earnestly seek to do right and be faithful. The thorns that prick, that stick in the flesh, that hurt, often change lives which seem robbed of significance and hope. In this way, the soul can become like soft clay in the hands of the Master in building lives of faith, usefulness, beauty, and strength. For some, the refiner's fire causes a loss of belief and faith in God, but those with eternal perspective understand that such refining is part of the perfection process."[4]*

John Taylor was one of the early prophets of The Church of Jesus Christ of Latter-day Saints. He saw enormous suffering during his lifetime. Death, sickness, poverty and betrayal among innocent saints. He said, *"I used to think, if I were the Lord, I would*

*not suffer people to be tried as they are. But I have changed my mind
on that subject. Now I think I would, if I were the Lord, because
it purges out the meanness and corruption that stick around the
Saints, like flies around molasses."*[5]

Still the world protests and wonders how the Lord can ask
so much. The Lord has responded, *"For my thoughts are not your
thoughts, neither are your ways my ways …"* (Isaiah 55:8).

We do not have the spiritual eyes to see all that He sees. But
we can rest assured in His promise. *"Peace I leave with you, my
peace I give unto you: not as the world giveth, give I unto you. Let not
your heart be troubled, neither let it be afraid"* (John 14:27).

By definition, our trials will be trying. There may be anguish,
confusion, sleepless nights, depression, anxiety, and pillows wet
with tears. But let us hold tight to our eternal perspective. Our trials
need not be spiritually fatal.[6]

Where can we fortify our understanding of this eternal
perspective? A good place to start is the scriptures. As we study,
the plan of salvation – the plan of happiness – becomes central
to everything else in the gospel. It gives meaning to life's roller
coaster. If we continue to trust in the Lord's word in scripture, it
will bring us closer to the happiness we are seeking. The Savior has
said, *"These things I have spoken unto you, that in me ye might have
peace. In the world ye shall have tribulation:* **but be of good cheer;** *I
have overcome the world"* (John 16:33).

Sometimes we must cling to our core belief even when doubts
scream at us from all sides. The world will find discrepancies that
attempt to tear holes in our testimonies. Distractions pull us away
from the fundamental gospel. But we can overcome by clinging
tight. The Lord has said that our belief is a critical piece of an
eternal promise. *"Search diligently, pray always,* ***and be believing,***

and all things shall work together for your good, if ye walk uprightly and remember the covenant wherewith ye have covenanted one with another" (D&C 90:24).

The scriptures are full of optimism. Stories and direction from the Lord to those in earlier times. We read, we ponder and we hope. At some point, you realize that you are not looking back at Jesus Christ's life, but that we have become present with Him. The scriptures are about now. It's the point when we realize He is present with us. And His grip is a lot stronger than ours.

As children of God we come from divinity. Nobility is in our soul. We were sent here to love and serve and lift others up. Learning and becoming more like Him in the process.

Each one of us has a part to play, and no matter how small or how insignificant you think your part is, it matters to the whole. We have something very important to do. We were born to lead and change the world.[7]

Life's battles try to stain the perception of ourselves. Soon we may forget. The truth is – it's not what you *are* that is holding you back. It's what you think you are *not*.

Think again.

We must dig deep. Look inside and remember our worth. Where we came from. And remember who we really are. Chogyam Trungpa said, *"The ultimate definition of bravery is not being afraid of who you are."*

We must learn to push past the negativity. Walls of rejection. Doubts both heard from others and felt within. It is finding and recognizing your gifts. There is something you can do to make a difference. People whose lives will change because you stepped up. It is conquering the fear that screams you can't. And trusting your faith that whispers you can.

One brave step forward. It's about finding a stronger partnership and focus – in Him. He is the ultimate guide. If you're on the wrong path, He will let you know. There will be dead ends. And if it is right, hang on tight. He will be your wings. Emerson agreed. *"What lies behind us and what lies before us are small matters compared to what lies within us."*

Recognize your worth. No matter where you live or what your circumstance. Lift your head. It holds a crown. Perhaps invisible to the world. But not to Him.

God is aware of our "once upon a time." He knows our story.

The plot thickens as characters are being developed. He knows all the words with the turns and twists that become our story. The joy. The laughter. The heartache and the tears.

Then storylines take us places we could not have imagined. New chapters and lessons become perfectly aligned. Just as He knew they would. Details of the story connecting in ways that enlighten and enrich. Every story a miracle.

This is the real fairy tale.

Chapters which take us to mountaintops where vision is clear and victory is realized. And chapters where eyes see the steep trail and we feel defeated and overwhelmed. Sometimes unable or unwilling to climb.

Each chapter won't define us. But they will shape us. Change us.

Where one chapter ends, another begins. A life-long process of learning to trust. Struggles becoming strengths. Developing eternal perspectives. And becoming more like Him. Recognizing the divinity within us and then learning to live it.

Remember where you've been. And who you're now becoming. Find your voice. Find your alleluia.

God will weep with joy as we turn the final page.

And they lived happily ever after.

Proud of our journey back to Him to a place more glorious than we can even imagine.

Until then, we live. Just like Servie lived – one chapter, one trial, one heartache at a time. Though she felt alone, she wasn't ever lonely. God is always there. He knows the beginning, the middle and the end. He knows the melody.

He knows *your* song.

Servie and husband Simon on their wedding day 1973

Thabani (first son) age 14

Thembelani (second son) age 15 receiving his math award

Left to right. Thembelihle
(second daughter),
Thandeka (first daughter)
and Thembelani (second
son)

Mlungisi (third son) age 8

Kimberly (third daughter)
age 2

Samkeliso (Servie's sister-in-law
who raised Kimberly) on far left
with Kimberly age 4

Simon (Servie's brother who
raised Kimberly)

Kimberly age 5

Sithabile (Servie's adopted
daughter) age 15

Angela

Angela and Servie

Servie on her baptism day

Kimberly with Angela receiving her U.S. citizenship

Servie and Kimberly

Servie and author Heidi Tucker

BOOK CLUB DISCUSSION QUESTIONS

Plot:

- Did you pick out any themes throughout the book?"
- Is the plot engaging—did you find the story interesting? Were you surprised by complications, twists and turns in Servie's life?
- What scene resonated most with you personally in either a positive or negative way? Why?
- What scene was the most pivotal for the book?

Characters:

- How did the characters change throughout the story? How did your opinion of them change?
- Are the main characters dynamic—changing or maturing by the end of the book?
- How has Servie inspired you?
- What do you learn from Angela?

Lessons:

- What did you learn from, take away from, or get out of this book?
- Have any of YOUR views or thoughts changed after reading this book?
- What passages strike you as insightful, even profound?
- What steps can you take to move forward in your own life and make a difference?

Experience:

- Did the book change your opinion or perspective about anything? Do you feel different now than you did before you read it?
- Have you read any other books by this author? Were they comparable to your level of enjoyment to this one?

NOTES

Introduction
www.neuschwanstein.de/englisch/palace/index.htm

Chapter 2 – Divine Nature
[1] R. Val Johnson, "South Africa: Land of Good Hope," Ensign, February 1993.
[2] Donald L. Hallstrom, "I Am a Child of God," General Conference, April 2016.
[3] Coleen K. Menlove, "Living Happily Ever After," General Conference, April 2000.
[4] Marvin J. Ashton, "A Yearning for Home," Ensign, November 1992.
[5] Thomas S. Monson, "He Is Risen!" Ensign, May 2010.
[6] James E. Faust, "What It Means to Be a Daughter of God," General Conference, October 1999.
[7] D. Todd Christofferson, "As Many as I Love, I Rebuke and Chasten," General Conference, April 2011.
[8] Helen Keller and Ray Silverman, "How I Would Help the World."
[9] Mary Ellen Smoot, "Embrace Your Wonderful Identity and Rejoice!" Open House, Fall 1999.
[10] Gordon B. Hinckley, "Live Up to Your Inheritance," Ensign, November 1983.

Chapter 3 – Live Your Truth
[1] D. Todd Christofferson, "As Many as I Love, I Rebuke and Chasten," General Conference, April 2011.
[2] Kenda Creasy Dean, "Almost Christian: What the Faith of Our Teenagers is Telling the American Church," Oxford University Press, 2010, p. 37.
[3] Russell M. Nelson, "A Plea to My Sisters," General Conference, October 2015.
[4] Julie B. Beck, "Strengthening Families by Increasing Spirituality," Ensign, September 2011.
[5] Neill F. Marriott, "What Shall We Do?" General Women's Conference, April 2016.
[6] Neal A. Maxwell, "Even As I Am," Shadow Mountain Press, 1982, p. 102.
[7] Neal A. Maxwell, "A Time to Choose," Deseret Book, 1972, p. 56.
[8] Vaughn J. Featherstone, "The Incomparable Christ: Our Master and Model," p. 135-136.
[9] Gospeldoctrine.com: Acts 20:19
[10] Elray L. Christiansen, "Conference Report," April 1953, p. 36.

[11] Dieter F. Uchtdorf, "Living the Gospel Joyful," General Conference, October 2014.

Chapter 4 – A Broken Heart
[1] Lance B. Wickman, "But If Not," Ensign, November 2002.
[2] James Montgomery, "Prayer Is the Soul's Sincere Desire," in Hymns of The Church of Jesus Christ of Latter-day Saints (Salt Lake City: The Church of Jesus Christ of Latter-day Saints, 1985), no. 145.
[3] Matthew 10:29
[4] Joseph B. Wirthlin, "Finding a Safe Harbor," Ensign, May 2000.
[5] Dennis E. Simmons, "But If Not ..." Ensign, May 2004.

Chapter 5 – Adjust Your Sails
[1] Danny Gokey, "Tell Your Heart to Beat Again," words and music, 2014.
[2] Anonymous.
[3] Brad Wilcox, "6 Childlike Traits that You've Probably Lost (And How to Get Them Back)," LDS Living, April 2014.
[4] James E. Faust, "The Refiner's Fire," General Conference, April 1979.
[5] Joseph B. Wirthlin, "Come What May, and Love It," Ensign, November 2008.
[6] Kevin R. Duncan, "The Healing Ointment of Forgiveness," General Conference, May 2016.
[7] Dieter F. Uchtdorf, "Your Happily Ever After," General Conference, April 2010.
[8] Brad Wilcox, "6 Childlike Traits that You've Probably Lost (And How to Get Them Back)," LDS Living, April 2014.
[9] William George Jordan, "Little Problems of Married Life," Improvement Era, July 1911.
[10] Thomas S. Monson, "Living the Abundant Life," Ensign, January 2012, p. 4.
[11] Laura Story, "Blessings," words and music, 2011.
[12] James E. Faust, "Womanhood: The Highest Place of Honor," Ensign, May 2000.
[13] Margaret D. Nadauld, "The Joy of Womanhood," General Conference, October 2000.
[14] Henry B. Eyring, "Trust in That Spirit Which Leadeth to Do Good," General Conference, April 2016.
[15] Coleen K. Menlove, "Living Happily Ever After," General Conference, April 2000.

Chapter 6 – A Song of Service
[1] Robert D. Hales, "Your Sorrow Shall Be Turned to Joy," General Conference, October 1983.
[2] Marion G. Romney, Conference Report, October 4, 1941, p. 89.

[3] Thomas S. Monson, "What Have I Done for Someone Today?" General Conference, October 2009.

[4] Cecil O. Samuelson, "Joy in the Divine Roles of Men and Women," BYU Speeches, April 29, 2004.

[5] Gordon B. Hinckley, "Whosoever Will Save His Life," Ensign, August 1982.

[6] Clark Cederlof, "Dignity," Gospel Reflections, 2000.

[7] Thomas S. Monson, "Three Goals to Guide You," General Conference, October 2007.

[8] Thomas S. Monson, "What Have I Done for Someone Today?" General Conference, November 2009.

[9] Dieter F. Uchtdorf, "You Are My Hands," General Conference, April 2010.

[10] Dieter F. Uchtdorf, "You Are My Hands," General Conference, April 2010.

Chapter 7 – Then Sings My Soul

[1] Spencer W. Kimball, "Are We Doing All We Can?" Ensign, February 1983.

[2] Thomas S. Monson, "Hopeless Dawn – Joyful Morning," Ensign, February 1993.

[3] Dallin H. Oaks, "Resurrection," Ensign, May 2000.

[4] Joseph Smith, History of the Church, Originally published 1932, Shadow Mountain Press, 1991, 1:282.

Chapter 8 – One Song

[1] Kevin W. Pearson, "Improving Your Personal Prayers," Ensign, June 2013.

[2] Richard G. Scott, "Trust in the Lord," General Conference, October 1995.

Chapter 9 – A Song of Hope

[1] Samuel Medley, "I Know That My Redeemer Lives," in Hymns of The Church of Jesus Christ of Latter-day Saints (Salt Lake City: The Church of Jesus Christ of Latter-day Saints, 1985), no. 136.

Chapter 10 – Your Song

[1] Dieter F. Uchtdorf, "Your Happily Ever After," General Conference, April 2010.

[2] Sheri L. Dew, "This Is a Test. It is Only a Test," The Best of Women's Conference, Deseret Book, January 2000.

[3] Neil L. Andersen, "Trial of Your Faith," General Conference, October 2012.

[4] James E. Faust, "The Refiner's Fire," General Conference, April 1979.

[5] John Taylor, "The Gospel Kingdom: Selections from the Writings and Discourses of John Taylor," Improvement Era, 1941.

[6] Neil L. Andersen, "Trial of Your Faith," General Conference, October 2012.

[7] Elaine S. Dalton, "Now Is the Time to Arise and Shine," General Conference, April 2012.

BIBLIOGRAPHY

Andersen, Neil L., "Trial of Your Faith." General Conference. October 2012.

Ashton, Marvin J., "A Yearning for Home." Ensign. November 1992.

Beck, Julie B., "Strengthening Families by Increasing Spirituality." Ensign. September 2011.

Cederlof, Clark, "Dignity." Gospel Reflections. 2000.

Christiansen, Elray L., Conference Report. April 1953.

Christofferson, D. Todd, "As Many as I Love, I Rebuke and Chasten." General Conference. April 2011.

Dalton, Elaine S., "Now Is the Time to Arise and Shine" General Conference. April 2012.

Dean, Kenda Creasy, Almost Christian: What the Faith of Our Teenagers is Telling the American Church. Oxford University Press 2010.

Dew, Sheri L., "This Is a Test. It is Only a Test." The Best of Women's Conference. Salt Lake City: Deseret Book. January 2000.

Eyring, Henry B., "Trust in That Spirit Which Leadeth to Do Good." General Conference. April 2016.

Faust, James E., "The Refiner's Fire." General Conference. April 1979.

Faust, James E., "What It Means to Be a Daughter of God." General Conference. October 1999.

Faust, James E., "Womanhood: The Highest Place of Honor." Ensign. May 2000.

Featherstone, Vaughn J., The Incomparable Christ: Our Master and Model. Salt Lake City: Deseret Book 2010.

Gokey, Danny, "Tell Your Heart To Beat Again." Words and music 2014.

Gospeldoctrine.com. Bryan Richards. Acts 20:19.

Hales, Robert D., "Your Sorrow Shall Be Turned to Joy." General Conference. October 1983.

Hallstrom, Donald L., "I Am a Child of God." General Conference. April 2016.

Hinckley, Gordon B., "Live Up to Your Inheritance." Ensign. November 1983.

Hinckley, Gordon B., "Whosoever Will Save His Life." Ensign. August 1982.

Johnson, R. Val, "South Africa: Land of Good Hope." Ensign. February 1993.

Jordan, William George, "Little Problems of Married Life." Improvement Era. July 1911.

Keller, Helen and Silverman, Ray, How I Would Help the World. West Chester: Swedenborg Foundation Press 2011.

Kimball, Spencer W., "Are We Doing All We Can?" Ensign. February 1983.

Marriott, Neill F., "What Shall We Do?" General Women's Conference. April 2016.

Maxwell, Neal A., A Time to Choose. Salt Lake City: Deseret Book 1972.

Maxwell, Neal A., Even As I Am. Salt Lake City: Shadow Mountain Press 1982.

Medley, Samuel, "I Know That My Redeemer Lives." Hymns of The Church of Jesus Christ of Latter-day Saints. Salt Lake City: The Church of Jesus Christ of Latter-day Saints, 1985.

Menlove, Coleen K., "Living Happily Ever After." General Conference. April 2000.

Monson, Thomas S., "He Is Risen!" Ensign. May 2010.

Monson, Thomas S., "Hopeless Dawn – Joyful Morning." Ensign. February 1993.

Monson, Thomas S., "Living the Abundant Life." Ensign. January 2012.

Monson, Thomas S., "Three Goals to Guide You." General Conference. October 2007.

Monson, Thomas S., "What Have I Done for Someone Today?" General Conference. October 2009.

Montgomery, James, "Prayer Is the Soul's Sincere Desire." Hymns of The Church of Jesus Christ of Latter-day Saints. Salt Lake City: The Church of Jesus Christ of Latter-day Saints 1985.

Nadauld, Margaret D., "The Joy of Womanhood." General Conference. October 2000.

Nelson, Russell M., "A Plea to My Sisters." General Conference. October 2015.

Neuschwanstein.de/englisch/palace/index.htm

Oaks, Dallin H., "Resurrection." Ensign. May 2000.

Pearson, Kevin W., "Improving Your Personal Prayers." Ensign. June 2013.

Romney, Marion G., Conference Report. October 1941.

Samuelson, Cecil O., "Joy in the Divine Roles of Men and Women." BYU Speeches. April 29, 2004.

Scott, Richard G., "Trust in the Lord." General Conference. October 1995.

Simmons, Dennis E., "But If Not ..." Ensign. May 2004.

Smith, Joseph, History of the Church. Originally published 1932. Salt Lake City: Shadow Mountain Press 1991.

Smoot, Mary Ellen, "Embrace Your Wonderful Identity and Rejoice!" Open House. Fall 1999.

Story, Laura, "Blessings." Words and music 2011.

Taylor, John, "The Gospel Kingdom: Selections from the Writings and Discourses of John Taylor." Improvement Era. 1941.

Uchtdorf, Dieter F., "Living the Gospel Joyful." General Conference. October 2014.

Uchtdorf, Dieter F., "You Are My Hands." General Conference. April 2010.

Uchtdorf, Dieter F., "Your Happily Ever After." General Conference. April 2010.

Wickman, Lance B., "But If Not." Ensign. November 2002.

Wilcox, Brad, "6 Childlike Traits that You've Probably Lost (And How to Get Them Back)." LDS Living. April 2014.

Wirthlin, Joseph B., "Finding a Safe Harbor." Ensign. May 2000.